A TASTE FOR BROWN BODIES

SEXUAL CULTURES

GENERAL EDITORS: Ann Pellegrini, Tavia Nyong'o, and
Joshua Chambers-Letson
FOUNDING EDITORS: José Esteban Muñoz and Ann Pellegrini

Titles in the series include:

God Hates Fags: The Rhetorics of Religious Violence
Michael Cobb

*Once You Go Black: Choice, Desire, and the Black
American Intellectual*
Robert Reid-Pharr

*The Latino Body: Crisis Identities in American Literary and
Cultural Memory*
Lázaro Lima

*Arranging Grief: Sacred Time and the Body in
Nineteenth-Century America*
Dana Luciano

Cruising Utopia: The Then and There of Queer Futurity
José Esteban Muñoz

Another Country: Queer Anti-Urbanism
Scott Herring

*Extravagant Abjection: Blackness, Power, and Sexuality in the
African American Literary Imagination*
Darieck Scott

Relocations: Queer Suburban Imaginaries
Karen Tongson

*Beyond the Nation: Diasporic Filipino Literature and
Queer Reading*
Martin Joseph Ponce

Single: Arguments for the Uncoupled
Michael Cobb

A Taste for Brown Bodies

Gay Modernity and Cosmopolitan Desire

Hiram Pérez

NEW YORK UNIVERSITY PRESS

New York and London

NEW YORK UNIVERSITY PRESS
New York and London
www.nyupress.org

© 2015 by New York University
All rights reserved

References to Internet websites (URLs) were accurate at the time of writing.
Neither the author nor New York University Press is responsible for URLs that
may have expired or changed since the manuscript was prepared.

ISBN: 978-1-4798-1865-5 (hardback)
ISBN: 978-1-4798-4586-6 (paperback)

For Library of Congress Cataloging-in-Publication data, please contact the
Library of Congress.

New York University Press books are printed on acid-free paper,
and their binding materials are chosen for strength and durability.
We strive to use environmentally responsible suppliers and materials
to the greatest extent possible in publishing our books.

Manufactured in the United States of America

10 9 8 7 6 5 4 3 2 1

Also available as an ebook

CONTENTS

ACKNOWLEDGMENTS

This book would not have seen the light of day without the (not always so gentle) prodding of Sarita See, dear sister friend and partner in crime since the Columbia days. The same is true for José Munoz's persistent solicitation—for his cornering me at conferences to inquire about the manuscript and insist that I send it to him. Like so many others, I owe José too much to account for here. In José, we lost not only a fierce and generous intellectual but also a great champion of queer of color scholars, even us resistant ones. I am hugely grateful also to friend and writing buddy Joseph Keith, who read and offered feedback on every part of this book and encouraged me through the rough patches. In addition to Joe and Sarita, a cohort of Columbia warriors has stood by me through the years, scarred but steadfast. They include Chris Cynn, Lisa Estreich, Amy Martin, and Yukari Yanagino. Chris has often served as an invaluable interlocutor for this project. For seeing me through Columbia when things looked bleak, many thanks to John Archer, Marcellus Blount, Kimberlé Crenshaw, David Eng, Farah Jasmine Griffin, Jean Howard, Kendall Thomas, and Patricia Williams.

Never one to do things the easy way, I owe a great debt to all the very patient friends who have stuck by me (and stuck up for me) over the course of my tumultuous academic career. Truly, I would be lost without you, Margaret Kent Bass, Janet Cutler, Chrissy Danguilan, Edvige Giunta, Jack Halberstam, Kim Hall, Kay Hallberg, David Lloyd, Patricia Matthew, Elaine Roth, Bill St. Amant, Jen Sinton, Peter Siriprakorn, Barbara Zubrickas. You are all very dear to me. Kim Hall in particular has done quite a bit of heavy lifting stewarding my career, often needing to outmaneuver my stubbornness. A shout out goes to my Miami crew, who always know how to make me laugh: Laura McDermott-Camp and Abel Santamaria.

I am endlessly grateful to Eve Dunbar and Kiese Laymon for all the work they do at Vassar, burning a righteous path for people like me and many others to follow. Their warmth, generosity, and fierceness have sustained me. Thanks to all my supportive Vassar friends and colleagues: Carlos Alamo, Marie Ausanio, Light Carruyo, Kristie Carter, Heesok Chang, Lisa Collins, Gunnar Danell, Wendy Graham, Maria Hantzopoulos, Luke Harris, Sophia Harvey, Hua Hsu, Luis Inoa, Jean Kane, Kenisha Kelly, Dorothy Kim, Molly McGlennen, Lydia Murdoch, Barbara Olsen, Karen Robertson, Paul Russell, Molly Shanley, Eva Woods, Susan Zlotnick. Vassar College has provided me with outstanding research assistants who have contributed significantly to the completion of this book. They include Cheikh Athj, Jeremy Garza, and Gustav Meuschke, three exciting young intellectuals to be reckoned with.

The series editors for Sexual Cultures saw this project through what was a difficult time of transition for them, and for that I remain deeply grateful. Thank you, Joshua Chambers-Letson, Tavia Nyong'o, and Ann Pellegrini. Working closely with Josh, whom I knew only by reputation beforehand, was especially rewarding. Many thanks as well to Eric Zinner and Alicia Nadkarni for their guidance and support throughout the process. I am grateful to the two anonymous reviewers who provided indispensible critiques.

I benefited immensely from the support I received at Princeton University's Center for African American Studies, where I was a Ford Postdoctoral Fellow. Quite frankly I needed that time to recuperate from the horror show of my early career. The friendships I formed there with Daphne Brooks, Judith Casselberry, Ricardo Montez, Noliwe Rooks, Alexandra Vazquez, and Judith Weisenfeld revived me more than they will ever know. I am especially grateful for the mentorship I received that year from the brilliant Valerie Smith. The completion of this project was also assisted by the generous support of the Susan Turner Fund administered by the Vassar College Committee on Research.

As I completed the book, I benefited from the wisdom and camaraderie of many old and new friends. Even when they were busy fighting their own battles, they made time for me. Thank you, Sadia Abbas, Alan Bass, Joseph Nicholas DeFilippis, Steven Fullwood, Eva Hageman, Lisa Kahaleole Hall, Christina Hanhardt, Keith Harris, Maja Horn, Eng-Beng Lim, Darnell Moore, Hoang Tan Nguyen, Joe Osmundson, Audra Simpson, Andrea Smith, Chi-ming Yang. You inspire me with the beauty and bravery of your scholarship, pedagogy, activism, and art.

Introduction

Queer studies, despite its critiques of normativity and its calls for a nonexclusionary politics, remains susceptible to forms of race unconsciousness—that is, subject to a racial unconscious shaped by nation, empire, and the dispositions of global capitalism, as well as resistant to the self-reflexive analytic standpoint that critical race theory advocates as "race consciousness." What can be more normative to modernity than whiteness? Is it even imaginable to think the erotic—and the homoerotic—without contemplating its intercourse with race? Sharon Holland recently has raised similar questions: "Can work on 'desire' be antiracist work? Can antiracist work think 'desire'? What would happen if we opened up the erotic to a scene of racist hailing?"[1] In addition to plotting an inside and out of queer theory, I present with *A Taste for Brown Bodies: Gay Modernity and Cosmopolitan Desire* a demystification of the primitive, exotic, or "brown" body commodified by dominant gay male culture. I propose regarding that brown body as an axis in the formation of a cosmopolitan gay male identity and community.

Queer theory, keenly attuned to the policing of desire, seemingly would provide an ideal field of inquiry for analysis into the racialized erotics of modernity. Yet the failures of queer theory to adequately address race are widely documented across the emergence of queer of color, postcolonial queer, black queer, indigenous queer, and queer diaspora critiques, among others. Hardly mere tributaries to queer theory, as Michael Warner would have us believe, these fields reinvigorate the very promises of queer as both a political movement and a hermeneutic.[2] *A Taste for Brown Bodies* takes up Holland's questions, particularly in regard to the place of white men's interracial same-sex desire and its brown objects as obligatory constituents of gay modernity. I am not interested in biographical accounts of interracial same-sex relations; more exactly, what interests me are biographies of desire and how a racialized homoerotic capacitates the imaginations of gay modernity. The question of desire's "traveling eye" necessarily calls into consideration technologies of mobility—both literal and imaginative—that move the subject, his body, and his desires. Those technologies include whiteness; however, the subject I isolate is not exclusively the white "gentleman traveler," as might be expected, but also a "trade" class consisting of merchant marines, so-called rogue soldiers, and cowboys, all of whom convey the brown body to the traveling eye of gay modernity. They do so through their legendary encounters with the primitive, by themselves embodying brownness (or modes of primitivity), and by acting as intermediaries for cosmopolitan identification. That the term "cosmopolitan" is more often reserved for the "gentleman traveler" belies the misrecognized role of these proletariat journeymen in populating an exotic imaginary with the bodies of their primitive encounters as well as with their own bodies. The whiteness of this proletariat cosmopolitan—this *trade*, if you will—is both real (acting on the world through the privileged mobility accrued by white masculinity—a cosmopolitan mobility that originates with the white body but can be mortgaged from it) and imagined (in the appropriation of historical figures, such as the black cowboy, who are whitewashed in order to assume a national masculinity and in fact a national sexuality).

Gay modernity's cathexis of the exotic traverses multiple routes of international trade. This fairly superficial historical observation, however, begs the question, what is the relationship of trade to *trade*—that is, the relation of international commerce to the proliferation of homosexual trade: rough trade, tearoom trade, military trade, and tomorrow's competition (née today's trade)?[3] We also might reframe this question to consider, more broadly, the relationship of political economies to a modern gay male subject—that infamous "personage" traced to the late nineteenth century by Michel Foucault, Eve Sedgwick, and numerous new historicists and queer scholars. I propose that *trade* (in their various hard and soft currencies) play a not-so-insignificant role in the development of the modern liberal nation-state. The marginalized situation of the homosexual authorizes modes of sexual exceptionalism that screen the historical collusions of U.S. empire and gay modernity, as do the peculiarly repressed queer pasts of such icons of U.S. masculinity as the sailor, the soldier, and the cowboy—collectively, the rough trade of U.S. imperialism. Neither gay liberation politics nor queer activism has ever fully reckoned with the tacit, if complex, participation of gay modernity in U.S. imperialist expansion. My objective is not recrimination but rather an injunction for queer critique to imagine alternative erotic cosmopolitanisms and to more rigorously interrogate how its institutionalizations (within academia, the nation, and liberalism, for instance) have compromised its radical political promise. Queer critique must investigate the circulation of homosexual desire within the erotic economies of both capitalism and the nation in order to guard against its cooptation into neoliberal and colonial projects. As Jasbir Puar pointedly remarks, "there is nothing inherently or intrinsically antination or antinationalist about queerness."[4]

The modern gay male subject remains inscribed in the nation's imperialist project in ways that require significant analytic disentangling. I propose that the modern gay male identity often traced to the late Victorian constructions of "invert" and "homosexual" occupies not the periphery of the nation but rather a cosmopolitan locus instrumental to projects of war, colonialism, and, ultimately, neoliberalism. Arguably himself a product of fin-de-siécle innovations in visual technology, the gay cosmopolitan also becomes an agent for colonial deployments of vision—and a predecessor to the gay neoliberal citizen-subject. A range of mobilities, transformed or generated by industrialization (i.e., class privilege, whiteness, transportation technology, mass media, leisure tourism) and, eventually, postindustrial society (i.e., communication and information technologies) all animate the cosmopolitanism of the modern gay male subject.

Jasbir Puar's thesis on homonationalism increasingly is cited beyond the fields of queer theory, gender studies, and postcolonial studies, to some degree challenging claims about the inaccessibility (or irrelevance) of queer scholarship. Focusing primarily on the early 1990s to the present—in terms of U.S. imperialism, a period framed by the First Gulf War and the ongoing "war on terror"—Puar's thesis characterizes homonationalism as a spatiotemporal network that dynamically links the nation's interests to lesbian, gay, and queer self-interests, so that "[t]hese proliferating sexualities, and their explicit and implicit relationships to nationalism, complicate the dichotomous implications of casting the nation as only supportive and productive of heteronormativity and always repressive and disallowing of homosexuality" (39). Likewise, the editors of the *Social Text* special issue "What's Queer about Queer Studies Now?" (2005) emphasize the neoliberal turn of the 1990s in a critique of "queer liberalism" contextualized within "a number of historical emergencies . . . of both national and global consequence,"[5] citing in particular political crises and debates defining the past two decades of American life (i.e., the dismantling of the welfare state, the "war on terror," the center-staging of competing religious fundamentalisms, the continued criminalization and pathologizing of immigrant bodies, etc.).

My argument builds on these critiques but also elaborates on them in two significant ways. First, I enlarge the historical context, shifting from the 1990s to the 1890s, from the millennium and the "war on terror" to the fin-de-siécle and the gilded age of U.S. imperialism. Second, while Puar's thesis on homonationalism and the critique of queer liberalism by the editors of "What's Queer about Queer Studies Now?" (David L. Eng, Judith Halberstam, José Esteban Muñoz) focus mostly (though not exclusively) on the collusions of lesbian, gay, and queer subjects with nationalism as mediated either through uncritical appeals to rights discourse or through uninterrogated racial and economic privilege, I extend this analysis to the homoerotics of the nation—the incitements, accommodations, and instrumentalizations of queer desires by the nation. The sweep of this analytic shift allows me to reformulate the emergence of gay modernity, attending to racial difference, the nation, and empire, all of which remain absent or embedded or at best parenthetical in the foundational accounts of a nascent homosexual personage in the writing of Foucault and Sedgwick. Without such an analytic shift, the presumably subjectless critique of queer grammar risks perpetually consigning racial difference to the parenthetical.

A pioneering work in queer studies, Eve Sedgwick's *Epistemology of the Closet* (1990) deems works by Herman Melville, Oscar Wilde, Marcel Proust, and Henry James as the "foundational texts of modern gay male identity."[6] Sedgwick gestures toward an "international bond" among these texts, a quality ultimately nullified by the nationalist tenets of canon formation (49). This "international canvas," mentioned in passing by Sedgwick, incites, I argue, newly mobile desires and a newly cathected sensibility that will be designated as "modern" and "gay." We need to consider what material conditions produce "modern gay" both as conjuctive descriptor and as subject. The emergence of a modern gay male subject requires—like Puar's homonational—a spatiotemporal field. He becomes his desires (a "personage" or "species," as Foucault explains), but those desires are animated by the attendant cultures of leisure time, the modernization of travel, and advances in visual technology (not the least of which was the invention of cinema). As a cosmopolitan consumer-citizen subject, his flânerie now traverses the globe, and where his body does not or cannot pass, his eye travels (his imagination capacitated and electrified by the aforementioned technologies of transport and vision).

I use "gay cosmopolitan" to designate a subject position originating with (but not limited to) a white, urban, leisure-class gay male whose desire is cast materially onto the globe at the close of the nineteenth century. I hypothesize that the gay modernity often traced to sexology's "invert" and "homosexual" does not neatly inhabit the margins of the nation, occupying instead a more complicated cosmopolitan condition auxiliary to colonial and neocolonial expansion.

Rather than continuing to understand the late Victorian invention of homosexuality as a moment of singular and absolute abjection, let us consider the possibility of the homosexual as a practical, if accidental, agent of neocolonial expansion (the geographies of which are redefined too by new visual and information technologies), serviceable both to modern nation building and to transnational flows of capital. John D'Emilio has argued that capitalism makes possible the conditions for a homosexual identity by creating, through wage labor, new spaces for socialization outside the family.[7] Let us consider then how homosexual desire circulates instrumentally, incited by and engendering the erotic economies of capitalism and the nation: trade qua trade, trade cum trade.

Linguist Paul Baker defines "trade" as "ostensibly heterosexual (often working-class) men who have sex with other men, but do not identify as gay."[8] However, usage of the term has remained fluid. As Baker explains, "trade, which denotes a casual sexual partner, can apply to someone who is ostensibly heterosexual (possibly a male prostitute), but can also mean someone who is gay and available for sex. A gay aphorism 'today's trade is tomorrow's competition' (Gardiner 1997: 223) implies that the sexual identity of 'trade' is unfixed" (*Polari*, 43). The etymology of the word "trade," especially its designation of a working-class subject, exemplifies the type of cosmopolitanism I distinguish as trade or proletarian cosmopolitanism. Although usage can be traced back to seventeenth-century England in the context of prostitution, a specifically homosexual context emerges from exchanges among merchant marines, actors, fairground workers, and criminal subcultures. Baker traces the expression "trade curtain" to merchant marine slang: "Sailors sometimes were eight to a berth and in order to maintain a degree of privacy during homosexual sex, they would hang a curtain round their bunk."[9]

The growth of the merchant marine, as an aspect of industrial capitalism, heralds also the decline of sailing vessels and their modes of sociality, heterotopic but also potentially utopic spaces of male labor and camaraderie in Herman Melville's fiction. The novella *Billy Budd* in fact opens with the narrator's nostalgic reverie for a "time before steamships." This nostalgia exemplifies the temporal aspect of Foucault's heterotopias, what Cesar Casarino terms "heterochronies." Casarino expands on Foucault's treatment of time in his reading of Melville:

> Melville's ships embody the following paradox: it is only from within the precipitous and disastrous flux of the history of modernity that one can turn a longing gaze back over the ruins of what has been destroyed, that one can brush that history against the grain. If Foucault's dictum was that the ship is the heterotopia par excellence, that dictum needs now to be reformulated: the ship is the heterochrony par excellence.[10]

Casarino's elaboration on Foucault, his notion of a heterochronology, extends just as readily to the modern histories of the soldier and the cowboy. Similar to the sailor, each also experiences displacements that occasion incompatibilities of time and space, instances of "the problematic of the synchronicity of the nonsynchronous" (Casarino 5).

The soldier, sailor, and cowboy, in addition to sharing similarly itinerant careers (they do much of the initial legwork, so to speak, for a gay cosmopolitan imagination), also share historically a predisposition for "a longing gaze back over the ruins of what has been destroyed." In other words, they share a predisposition for nostalgia, as both subjects and objects of nostalgic desire. Queer scholarship has focused on these figures as icons of archetypal masculinity, personalities desired and "cloned" through a complex of (dis)identifications. The recovery of their queer pasts, lost to the sanctioned amnesia of the nation, is overdue.

Nostalgia characterizes the modern gay male subject's emergence in the late nineteenth century, constituting perhaps the signal modernity of his persona. A history of the idea of nostalgia is instructive in that its etymology, like that of the word "homosexual," traces back to medical discourse. Among the detrimental effects ascribed to nostalgia by early medical researchers, according to Svetlana Boym, was a "propensity for suicide," a susceptibility that will come to plague homosexual definition as well.[11] As Boym explains, nostalgia emerges during an era of mass displacements: "Unlike melancholia, which was regarded as an ailment of monks and philosophers, nostalgia was a more 'democratic' disease that threatened to affect soldiers and sailors displaced far from home as well as many country people who began to move to the cities" (5). This latter move described by Boym, from rural to urban, finds a twentieth-century correlation in the dominant narratives for gay male identity, traced to the gay man's relocation from the small town to the metropolis and metaphorized as "coming out." Yet if we persist in reading canonical narratives of gay identity through Boym's nostalgia, we find that he does not locate the object of his desire upon arriving in the city; rather, that union seems impossibly deferred. The metropolitan may return to the country, but his nostalgia, according to Boym, is not cured. Gloria Anzaldúa famously quipped in *Borderlands* that homophobia is the fear of going home. If we assume, for the sake of argument, that the modern gay male inherits the disposition of the nostalgic, then perhaps the homosexual is a figure who forever longs for home, a home that remains elusive both spatially and temporally.

The Swiss physician Johannes Hofer coined the word "nostalgia" in 1688 to describe the pathologically nonsynchronous experiences of displaced peoples, especially "Swiss soldiers fighting abroad" (Boym 3). Nostalgia, it turns out, is a peculiarly modern problem. Among the qualities that perplexed its earliest students was its apparent communicability. It affected not only isolated individuals but became also a common condition of entire populations. Boym links the development of nostalgia, and its particular congealment in the nineteenth century, to the irreversible notion of time that accompanied industrial progress. The same processes of industrialization that served to universalize the notion of progress facilitated greater opportunities for travel that then exposed the unevenness of progress. "Nostalgic manifestations are side effects of the teleology of progress." Boym continues: "Travelers since the late eighteenth century wrote about other places, first to the south and then to the east of Western Europe, as 'semi-civilized' or outright 'barbarous.'

Instead of coevalness of different conceptions of time, each local culture therefore was evaluated with regard to the central narrative of progress" (10). An irretrievable past ultimately romanticized onto the figure of the primitive (or what I designate as the "brown body") continues to shape modern gay sensibilities. A nostalgic mode of identification defines gay cosmopolitanism, animating exotic mise-en-scènes fundamental to the emergence and perpetuation of gay modernity and its complicities with U.S. empire.

Iconic figures of American masculinity such as the sailor, the cowboy, and the soldier represent enduring objects of queer desire, prototypes for subcultures of gay clones.[12] Although these figures are memorialized (and desired) for their heroic masculinity, their own queer histories dissipate under the erasure of the nation's sanctioned amnesia. In *A Taste for Brown Bodies*, I trace the foundations of gay modernity to queer cosmopolitanism, including the unexpectedly queer, proletarian cosmopolitanism of sailors, soldiers, and cowboys. Effectively screened by archetypal masculinities as well as, ironically, by their status as gay clones (achieved through the *dis*identifications of modern gay men), the queer cosmopolitanism of these figures was deployed to sustain and expand U.S. empire. Gay cosmopolitanism, crucial to the formation of gay modernity, has remained available to the enlistments of empire. It is crucial then to recover these routes of queer cosmopolitanism in order to understand the links between gay modernity and imperialism, links revealed for example by scholarship on the relation between neoliberalism and homonormativity. As Anna Agathangelou, Daniel Bassichis, and Tamara Spira spell out, "the violence and death we authorize and face operate through and within our libidinal, erotic, and affective investments, investments that we must engage directly and rigorously if we are to disrupt the seductive workings of power in their most intimate dimensions."[13] If a racialized homoerotics converges with U.S. empire to consolidate gay modernity, as I argue, then gay men committed to antiracist, leftist critiques are obligated to disentangle their own "intimate investments" from the projects of U.S. imperialism.

Queer studies provides me at once with a case study of racist practice and a methodology to identify and combat racism, particularly in its imbrication with the erotic. For instance, the University of Michigan's Gay Shame conference in 2003 (explored further below and in chapter 4) demonstrated the aggressive resistance of establishmentarian queer theory to thinking about race and power while also productively, if inadvertently, demonstrating the role of the brown body vis-à-vis gay modernity, albeit in ways that were at that time excruciating for several audience members (myself included). The conference enacted in painful ways gay modernity's desire for and dependence upon the brown body as an axis for a privileged gay male individuation and socialization, as well as the ways in which queer studies—itself also a mode of gay male sociality—aggressively defends, disavows, and disarticulates that relationship. I agree with Sharon Holland's recent observation that "we have uncoupled our desire from quotidian racist practice for far too long" (42). Gay male sociality, including queer theory, stages quotidian racist practices. While this hardly seems controversial, it often remains surprisingly difficult for queer studies to historically appraise its own erotic investments with race and power.

I initiate just such an appraisal here by tracing how a male same-sex erotics may be unexpectedly mobilized by practices of settler colonialism and neo-imperialism that simultaneously repudiate queer desire. By "erotics" I mean broadly those libidinal and affective economies that we designate as desire, pleasure, intimacy, seduction, and in some cases even repulsion or shame.[14] While expanding our vocabulary on the erotic and its relation to power, queer theory has participated at times in securing the transparency of whiteness, jettisoning questions of race as retrograde and provincial. While certainly marginalized vis-à-vis normative, national sexualities, a racialized homoerotics nonetheless was cultivated through late-nineteenth-century forms of industry and capitalism that not only generated increased mechanisms for mobility, especially for elite men, but also hastened U.S. expansionism.

Queer scholars and activists must interrogate the various potential complicities of dominant gay male sociality both to nation building and to global capitalism; otherwise, the "predatory" violences of these systems also operate across our bodies.[15] I am interested not only in how expansion was realized but also in how it was visualized, for and through gay men. In particular I interrogate the correspondence among looking outward (travel and expansion), looking inward (the secret), and looking backward (nostalgia), modes of visuality and in(di)visuality that gay modernity both required and proliferated.

Beginning with Eve Sedgwick's claim in *Epistemology of the Closet* that "an understanding of virtually any aspect of modern Western culture must be, not merely incomplete, but damaged in its central substance to the degree that it does not incorporate a critical analysis of homo/heterosexual definition" (1), queer theory has rigorously evaluated and contested the entrenched nature of heteronormativity in all kinds of social and cultural institutions. But only recently has queer theory turned its attention to the institutionalizing of "homonormativity" and more recently still, thanks to Jasbir Puar's *Terrorist Assemblages*, to affects and practices of "homonationalism."[16] For Puar, "homonationalism" instances a "brand of homosexuality" committed "to the global dominant ascendancy of whiteness that is implicated in the propagation of the United States as empire" (2). Both terms have been applied primarily to describe the neoliberal turn in gay and lesbian politics and culture beginning in the 1990s. I consider alternatively the possibility of an enduring homonationalism dating to the emergence of the homosexual in the late nineteenth century. *A Taste for Brown Bodies* examines how U.S. empire not only makes possible certain articulations of gay modernity but also instrumentalizes them. Empire and gay modernity in this sense become mutually propagating. This is not to say that the male homosexual occupies a "normative" position, a center of power, but it is to say that we need to complicate the margins. What I argue is that certain practices and subjectivities that we might understand historically as forms of homosexuality are regulated and normalized in their service to U.S. empire. Indeed, the particular propagation of the United States as empire that I examine is one that necessitates the margin; its extralegal operations require and deploy an outlaw sexuality. The enterprises of the cowboy, "rogue" soldier, and merchant marine often only tenuously obligate them to the nation-state, however much they later may be variously recuperated as icons of national masculinity. Nonetheless, all three figures have also functioned, officially and unofficially, as cosmopolitan extensions of the U.S. nation-state and as agents for the expansion of its borders and neocolonial zones of influence.

In framing my study, I return to the late nineteenth century also to trace capital's privatization as it extends to the self in the production of homosexual particularity. That particularity is grounded initially and perhaps most powerfully through pathologization but ultimately extends as well into the late twentieth century through the adoption by a mainstreamed gay liberation movement of discourses of liberation and freedom that celebrate the individual and his or her right to privacy. The reduction of freedom to privatized space (whether that of the bedroom or that of the individual psyche) ironically reifies the closet, in this case not only as the space of shamed (internalized) gay sexuality but also as an exclusionary space that defends a privileged and particularized homosexuality from consideration of its interdependency with class, race, and gender formations, hence inhibiting a more totalizing analysis and the political possibilities of coalition building. Such is the case with the gay cosmopolitanism at the Gay Shame conference that I critique in chapter 4 and in the global queer cinema represented by Tomás Gutiérrez Alea's *Fresa y chocolate*, discussed in chapter 3. However critical queer theory remains of mainstreamed, assimilationist gay politics, it shares a certain nostalgia for the particularized closet I describe. The mobility of the gay cosmopolitan, whether it be the more contingent, working-class kind of the soldier or the privileged variety of what Joseph Massad calls the "gay international," presents a constitutive quality of gay modernity.[17] The reification of a homosexual personage depends on this cosmopolitanism. Uninterrogated, gay modernity's cosmopolitanism elaborates itself, including—and often characteristically—in queer theoretical approaches. Hence, I extend the critiques offered by scholars like Duggan and Puar beyond the homonormative to modern homosexuality itself as a normalized practice in the margins of but instrumental to U.S. empire.

Writing primarily in the contexts of the Anglophone Caribbean and the United States, M. Jacqui Alexander (2006) argues that modern state apparatuses generate a regulatory heterosexualization at once necessary to the state's reproduction (ideologically, materially) but also intrinsically unstable, one might say "productive," in the Foucauldian sense. Following Jonathan Goldberg, Alexander traces sexual modernity to Balboa's mass execution of six hundred "sodomites" in a Panamanian village, inscribing notions of perversity onto imperialism and onto the racialized difference between savagery and civilization. The nation-states that emerge from settler colonialism remain ghosted by perverse origins, defending a normative heterosexuality derivative of sodomy. These origins in fact need to be perpetually sublimated, redirected, reinstrumentalized. What Alexander identifies as the constitutive paradox of heterosexualization provides a critical point of departure for my own analysis. Where Alexander inquires into the role of heterosexualization within the state apparatus, I ask instead about the imperial state's instrumentalized homosexualization, particularly in its deployments of what new historicists designate as modern gay male identity.

Puar's critique of homonationalism develops at least in part through her scholarship on queer tourism. Following her work on a special issue of *GLQ* devoted to "Queer Tourism: Geographies of Globalization" (2002), Puar contributed the essay "A Transnational Feminist Critique of Queer Tourism" to the journal *Antipode*. One of the primary objectives of the essay is "to tease out the neocolonial impulses of all queer travel by highlighting the colonial history of travel and tourism and the production of mobility through modernity and vice versa" (937). She builds here on M. Jacqui Alexander's groundbreaking work, and in particular

Alexander's argument that "white gay capital follows the path of white heterosexual capital," in order to ascertain in her own critique of tourism how "queer women, queers of color, and postcolonial lesbian[s] and gays [are] implicated in this process" (937). One of the primary objectives in *A Taste for Brown Bodies* is to test the hypothesis that white gay capital may in fact *clear* a path in service to white heterosexual capital. Like Puar, I too am interested in how modernity is linked to mobility in ways that complicate "white." For this reason, my deployment of "brownness" remains deliberately slippery, referring to bodies perceived, or at least described, literally as brown but also to the fantasies about racial and sexual others who fascinate modern gay male identity with their instinctive, earthy, volatile, scatological, savage, and dirty allure. In fact, the link here between "brownness" as a simultaneously abject and idyllic primitive condition and "brown" as racial vernacular (say, for Latino, Arab, Mediterranean, immigrant, terrorist, taxi driver, or "banjee boy") should immediately suggest symbolic origins for all racial difference signified by color (yellow, red, black, brown, white). This seems obvious enough, yet our tendency to intellectually underestimate the cruder aspects of racialization functions only to screen their monumental influence at the levels of both individual consciousness and a popular imaginary.

Puar links the decriminalization of homosexuality in the United States to mass consumption and the globalized markets of late capitalism:

> As a result of fears that labor will be able to traverse international boundaries as easily as capital does, globalization is increasingly responded to through heightened national border policings of various kinds (Alexander 1997). Within this context, gay and lesbian tourism is an ironic marker of an elitist cosmopolitan mobility, a group momentarily decriminalized through its purchasing power while immigrants are increasingly criminalized and contained. (942)

Puar's analysis is striking for many reasons, including the continued link between a gay cosmopolitan and a criminalized, "browned" body.

My interests within this study, in many ways similar to those of Puar and Alexander, differ in my concern with the emergence of gay male modernity and the scholarship of queer theory that traces that origin in ways that potentially obscure and collude with the inequities of power and mobility described above by Puar. An elitist gay and lesbian cosmopolitanism may not be so momentary, may provide a pivotal as well as ironic counterpart to criminalized brown migrations, and may in some epochs colonize space in service to the converging interests of the nation and capitalism. The most significant way in which *A Taste for Brown Bodies* diverges from Puar's and Alexander's projects is in my return to nineteenth-century monopoly capitalism as an imperialistic cultural foundation necessary to the formation of "gay male modernity" (a historical demarcation that I argue in some ways proves redundant). Secondly, I point to how a reconsideration, through queer of color analysis, of foundational and canonical gay texts such as Herman Melville's *Billy Budd* shifts the emphasis from the elite cosmopolitan to cosmopolitan trade in the figures of colonial labor traversing and securing anxious national, cultural, and bodily boundaries.[18] The seemingly accidental if inequitable relation between elite gays and criminalized migrant bodies (displaced overwhelmingly by globalized markets and the neocolonial politics of receiving nations) provides in my study a pivotal dynamic of eroticized racialization, one that is surprisingly destabilizing. Hence, I argue in chapter 1 that Herman Melville's obsessive attention to Billy Budd's whiteness ultimately marks the character's brownness. That brownness is narrativized through a familiar trope of orphaned identity that so commonly raises the specter of racial indeterminacy (exotic or miscegenous) in U.S. and British cultural production but perhaps more significantly through Billy Budd's situation as a merchant marine, crossing international waters not as an elite gay tourist but as a stuttering subaltern. In addition to tracing how gay male identity has been variously instrumentalized by the nation and by capitalism, I also inquire into how gay modernity makes some identities unintelligible in the process of canonizing others as proper liberal subjects.

I suggest then an alternative formation of homonationalism in the nineteenth century and trace its legacy to the present neoliberal moment of gay and queer assimilation. Alexander and Puar argue that white heterosexual capital invites and accommodates white gay capital in the late twentieth century; I propose a longstanding synergy among capital, whiteness, and homoerotic nationalism. What if homo- and heterosexual capital functioned concomitantly to reinforce and secure racial boundaries at home (defining a modern national culture) and to locate the primitive, sexual other abroad, at the margins of the nation's boundaries, or in occupied and/or international spaces often symbolically designated liminal (i.e., spaces of disputed or disregarded national sovereignty)? Modern gay male identity, at its foundation, I argue, is not so clearly peripheral or abject vis-à-vis the center. Its situation is much more fluid and ambiguous, flirting from the very start with heterosexual masculinities. Icons of celebrated national masculinity—such as the cowboy, the sailor, and the soldier—boast complex and contradictory sexual histories.

The cowboy, for instance, is enduringly romanticized, first by dimestore fiction and then by Hollywood, as the West's knight errant, a figure of unshakeable virtue in a lawless region of brown savagery (dusty Indians and Mexicans; queer, mustache-twirling ladykillers dressed in black; castrated or debauched "Orientals"; and foreign speculators, typically effete and unsuited to the rugged frontier terrain). However, as I detail in my closing chapter on *Brokeback Mountain*, the cowboy begins his career as a cattle thief and outlaw figure in many ways queer. Yet it is precisely his queerness that becomes serviceable to the nation in a project of westward expansion. He performs the dirty, unseen labor of Manifest Destiny—unseen in that his heroic cultural recuperation in the twentieth century obscures a violent outlaw past.

A Taste for Brown Bodies traces to unexpected figures the circulation of homosexual desire within the erotic economies of the nation and empire. I assess the legacy of gay cosmopolitanism in contemporary articulations of gay identity and queer "anti-identity." This book is my modest contribution to a literary and cultural genealogy of gay cosmopolitanism, without which, I argue, contemporary antiracist queer politics remains imperiled.

I begin in chapter 1, "The Queer Afterlife of *Billy Budd*," with a return to Herman Melville's *Billy Budd, Sailor: An Inside Narrative*, acknowledging Eve Sedgwick's evaluation of the novella as a text foundational to understanding modern gay male identity. The numerous twentieth-century adaptations of *Billy Budd* testify to its canonical significance to gay modernity. The African sailor, the narrative's original (originary) beautiful sailor, mediates same-sex desire in the novella as both a highly sensual and a highly nostalgic figure. I use the notion of the primitive, brown body to locate that ambiguous but charged fantastic object that cathects Victorian male same-sex desire into modern gay male identity. Billy Budd's primitive body, the object of Lieutenant Claggart's disowned desire, requires the confluence of global naval and commercial expansion (within the narrative, Billy moves from merchant vessel to a naval ship) together with histories of colonialism and slavery (that account for the presence of the story's African sailor in Liverpool). Furthermore, the narrative's resistant identification with Claggart is both mediated and disavowed through its comparison of Claggart to the Native American Tecumseh.

Billy Budd and the African sailor become unknowing architects of the closet. The narrative's homosexual desire is never entirely displaced onto Billy, as the African sailor remains the original fetish, the original "beautiful sailor." In that space between the African sailor's blackness and Billy's pallor (which we might read either as colorlessness—an allegorical veiling of blackness—or as rosiness, the allegorical blush of innocence), desire stirs backward, into the preindustrial "time before steamships" and onto the primitive body. The novella's constant deferral of desire, both in the form of the narrative and in the figure of the sexually frustrated Claggart, ironically constructs a model of autonomy for gay modernity in constituting its interiority, what Eve Sedgwick will identify as an epistemological closet. The "inside story" is a foundational account of gay interiority. Performative in its labyrinthine turns and evasions, the novella epitomizes Sedgwick's epistemological closet. *Billy Budd*, as a narrative, is the secret that begs to get told again and again, adapted numerous times across various mediums for over a century despite its performatively abstruse prose. The secret may not be articulated exactly, but it will be staged and visualized repeatedly.

The brown body reappears in chapter 2, "'Going to Meet the Man' in Abu Ghraib," as the sodomitical (or Saddamitical) bodies of Iraqi men incarcerated and tortured at Abu Ghraib. In order to link domestic regimes of race with U.S. imperialism, I turn to James Baldwin's short story "Going to Meet the Man" for an optic that insists on reading the Abu Ghraib archive as symptomatic of a racialized homoerotic of the nation. Baldwin's story suggests a rescripting of Freud's oedipal scene, introducing the black male as a triangulating figure vis-à-vis the (white) male child's identification with each parent. Hence, for Baldwin, fantasies about black male sexuality necessarily mediate the resolution of the oedipal complex in the American scene. A desire both to possess and to be possessed by the black man, to annihilate and be annihilated by him, functions to consolidate white indivisibility across the division of heterosexual and homosexual identifications that resolves the oedipal. I extend Baldwin's reading of this race secret to the abuses that occurred at the Abu Ghraib military prison not only in order to better understand the racialized and sexual nature of the violence but also to determine what about it was symptomatically American. I ask how the race secret in this instance is cast violently onto the globe and consider how digital technology restructures colonialism's field of vision.

I explore both the value and the limitations of a comparative analysis of lynching (and lynching photography) next to the abuses of Abu Ghraib (and the digital photographs of those abuses). My contention is that the domestic race secret—for Baldwin, the white man's desire for the black male body, regardless of sexual orientation—is globalized via U.S. neocolonialism. This casting of the American race secret onto the globe recruits a gay cosmopolitan archive, especially in its imagination of the exotic, or "brown" (in this case, Arab, Middle Eastern, Mediter-ranean, Muslim, "Oriental"). Jonathan Goldberg's reading of popular culture imagery of Saddam Hussein in the introduction to his book *Sodometries: Renaissance Texts, Modern Sexualities*, published in 1992, shortly after the Gulf War, seems prophetic today. Goldberg identifies fantasies, common to both English Renaissance and contemporary U.S. cultures, attributing specific sexual vices to regions broadly demarcated as "the Mediterranean" and "Islam." The reading that Goldberg provides of a November 1990 *Rolling Stone* ad for a t-shirt bearing an image of Saddam Hussein's face superimposed over a camel's ass, his mouth tak-ing the place of the camel's asshole, gives the lie to George W. Bush's case that the actions of the "rogue" U.S. soldiers at Abu Ghraib are in-congruous with the American way. In response to the Abu Ghraib con-troversy, Bush expressed disgust, describing the photos as an aberration of national values: "Their treatment does not reflect the nature of the American people. That's not the way we do things in America" (Stout). The responses from both the Pentagon and the White House invoke a "perpetrator perspective" all too familiar to students of U.S. racialism.[19] In other words, they attribute the torture, characterized as anomalous, to isolated (and deviant) individuals; U.S. race ideology and the failures of racial justice at home move onto the world stage. I argue that the torture (and the vexed nature of its "mechanical reproduction") does in-deed reflect something deeply American despite the president's protest. A national unconscious seizes on the brown body as a site onto which it can project the "unnatural" sex acts it disavows. This hegemonic imagi-nation has traditionally cast the Arab as sodomite. The stills, generated from army intelligence film shot at the prison as well as from digital photographs circulated by soldiers as electronic forms of the postcard, underscore cosmopolitanism's serviceability to military occupation through its archive of material and imagined travels. In other words, a tradition of gay cosmopolitanism provides the mise en scène for the Abu Ghraib photos. My reading of Baldwin reveals not only homosociality at the consolidation of white masculinity but also homoeroticism.

Chapter 3, "The Global Taste for Queer," traces a similar homosociality and homoeroticism in the anxious nationalist rhetoric of José Martí's
"Nuestra America," an essay first published in Mexico and completed
while the Cuban patriot lived in exile in New York City. Focusing on
Martí's treatment of racial hybridity, I argue that the miscegenation that
produces Martí's mestizo America is in fact a metaphorical miscegenation occurring between men. Hence, we again encounter an iteration of
homoeroticism as the locus of nation founding, in this instance sublimated within Martí's baroque prose. The baroque quality of the prose, as
I argue, itself may contain in fact another queer stratum to the postcolonial founding of the Cuban nation. Reading Tomas Gutiérrez Alea's film
Fresa y chocolate (1993) next to Martí's essay, I explore the entanglements
of race and sexuality in each text. I consider how gay male spectatorship
in the United States projects a problematic variety of cosmopolitanism
onto the film; alternatively, I insist on reading the film within its more
local context, situating it as a contemporary expression of Martí's foundational yet anxious nationalism. In other words, U.S. spectators may
not be wrong to recover Gutiérrez Alea's film as a text that is cosmopolitan in its queerness, but they misrecognize their own aggressively
universalized model of gay identity in the film's specifically Cuban contexts. The film's articulation of modern *Cuban* gay identity originates
in a cosmopolitan model, that of Martí's anticolonial and hemispheric
dialectics.

According to Joseba Gabilondo, a "global taste" for "queer" film
characterizes the international film market during the 1990s. In effect,
he identifies a film archive of gay cosmopolitanism, including *Fresa y
chocolate* in the catalogue of global queer cinema produced outside Hollywood, together with such works as *The Crying Game* (1992), *Farewell
My Concubine* (1993), *The Adventures of Priscilla, Queen of the Desert* (1994), and *Madame Butterfly* (1995). Insisting on reading *Fresa y
chocolate* within the multiple contexts of its global, local, and alternative
cosmopolitan (hemispheric and anticolonial) meaning making, I build
on Gabilondo's argument that these films negotiate "different national

situations and globalization . . . us[ing] the same discursive strategy of mobilizing a desiring male queer character in order to relegitimize and articulate a new global hegemony around the different national masculinities and hegemonies set in crisis by globalization" (236–37). The theme of seduction in *Fresa y chocolate*—the gay Diego's seduction of the communist youth, David—mirrors both the project of reconciliation to which the Cuban state deployed the film internationally as well as the Anglo American projection of erotic desire onto a fetishized Cuba. The global taste for queer cinema then directs us back to modern gay male identity's need for and production of the brown body.

In the fourth chapter—"You Can Have My Brown Body and Eat It, Too!"—I expand on my notion of the primal "brown body" mediating gay modernity. I argue that this brown body (frequently embodied as "Latino") mediates gay male shame. Andy Warhol's film, *Screen Test #2*, Douglas Crimp's essay on that film, "Mario Montez, For Shame," and the Gay Shame conference held at the University of Michigan in 2003, which opened with a showing of the Warhol film, provide the primary texts for my analysis. Crimp (and Gay Shame, by extension) deploys monolithic constructions of "Puerto Rican" and "Catholic" in order to project and universalize (the urbane, white gay man's) shame onto Montez's othered (or browned) body. I argue that Montez, rather than merely providing the passive object of Warhol's experiments in camera technique and exposure, skillfully pirates the film's authority in ways that remain illegible to Crimp's construction of gay shame. His performance works to shift the film's scrutiny—its discomfiting modes of exposure—alternately onto Warhol, Ronnie Tavel (Warhol's collaborator, off screen), and the spectator. I conclude the chapter by considering critiques of my original response to the conference.

In chapter 5, "Gay Cowboys Close to Home," I queer the nation-founding iconicity of the cowboy in the U.S. imagination. The chapter reviews what became a common critical reading of Ang Lee's *Brokeback Mountain* (2005) as "not a gay movie." I contest the prevailing reading of Ennis Del Mar as repressed homosexual, instead inviting his difference to help open both "gay" and "queer" to new narratives. Ennis's queerness is concentrated unexpectedly in the cowboy ethic that guides his life; because nationally that ethic is memorialized as heroically and uniquely masculine, its queerness has dissipated from legend. This chapter restores the queer in cowboy, insisting that we situate Ennis close to home (Wyoming, ranch labor, rural) in order to appreciate his difference. Hence, I challenge a metanarrative for modern gay identity largely founded on migration—to metropolitan locales, such as New York and San Francisco—and on a certain gay cosmopolitanism. Readings that characterize Ennis as either "repressed," "closeted," or "not gay" often resort to a cosmopolitan logic that then situates Jack as properly gay. What these readings fail to account for are the socioeconomic and geographic differences that estrange the characters as the story develops. Jack's greater mobility, especially his ability to travel outside the boundaries of the nation (as a sex tourist in Mexico), contributes to an articulation of sexuality that many viewers more readily label as "gay."

In contrast to most readings of the film, mine turns to both Annie Proulx's story and Lee's cinematic adaptation to critique gay assimilationism and the prioritizing of same-sex marriage in contemporary neoliberal ("homonormative") gay and lesbian politics. It is precisely Ennis's refusal to accommodate Jack's demands for domesticity that encourages gay assimilationists to read Ennis as closeted (even "cowardly") and Jack as tragically heroic. I locate the narrative's queerness not in Jack's domestic longing but rather in Ennis's nostalgia. *Brokeback Mountain* is all about queer space and time. It is the place where two "high school dropout country boys with no prospects" (256) scratch out a time "when they owned the world and nothing seemed wrong" (255). Ultimately, Jack Twist embraces a bourgeois lifestyle. While Jack Twist memorializes Brokeback Mountain as a rehearsal for marriage, Ennis Del Mar regards Brokeback Mountain, through a critical nostalgia and in classic cowboy style, as a circumvention and postponement of the law, as a queer space and time.

We find then in queer cultural production (including queer theorizing, such as that exemplified by Gay Shame) competing nostalgias, critical and reactionary. And in these figures of the cowboy, soldier, and sailor—as both subjects and objects of queer desire—we encounter the cultural mediation of nostalgias, critical but more often reactionary. These figures also perform colonial labor for a cosmopolitan desire that I argue is fundamental to gay modernity, a desire for the primitive, the exotic, the brown body. That desire, I argue, is excited, accommodated, and instrumentalized by U.S. empire in ways that remain undertheorized.

1

The Queer Afterlife of *Billy Budd*

A habitually nostalgic identificatory mode defines the gay cosmopolitan imagination, staging exotic mise en scènes vital to the emergence
and perpetuity of gay modernity and its collusions with U.S. empire.
Throughout this study, I refer to the "brown" body in order, among other
reasons, to signal the fluidity and racial ambiguity at work in the way a
gay cosmopolitan imagines an idealized primitive figure that functions
both as an object of desire and as the repository of disowned projections cast temporally and spatially backward. However, in framing my
analysis, especially in returning to new historicist arguments that trace
the origins of a modern gay male identity to the late nineteenth century,
I find myself continually thinking about blondness—odd, considering
my emphasis on the brown body and exoticist or primitivist fantasies.
If we follow Eve Sedgwick in privileging Herman Melville's *Billy Budd,
Sailor: An Inside Narrative* and Oscar Wilde's *Picture of Dorian Gray*
as foundational gay texts, it is the image of youthful blond beauty that
is celebrated and not that of the dusky exotic. My contention is that
blondness figures in these foundational texts as a queer proxy for primi-
tiveness. Dorian Gray and Billy Budd each activate an atavistic desire
within their respective narratives, each perpetuating the fantasy of child
savage, one cynical and the other naïve. Dorian's cynical primitivism is
mediated through the novel's orientalism, while Billy's naïve primitivism
requires the surrogacy of an African double, a mechanism consistent
with what Toni Morrison has termed the Africanist presence in U.S. literature, characteristic in particular of the American Renaissance.[1]

I focus in this chapter on Melville's novella because of its remarkable
queer afterlife in adaptation, across diverse media and national boundaries, including a novel by Jean Genet, which then inspires Rainer Werner

Fassbinder's final film by the same title, *Querelle*, an opera by Benjamin Britten (with libretto by E. M. Forster), Claire Denis's visually stunning film *Beau Travail*, which in turn inspires the pornographic video *Legionnaires* (directed by Jean-Marc Prouveur of Oh Man! Studios), and numerous pop culture citations, including a song by former Smiths frontman and international gay icon, Morrissey. By linking forms of gay male sociality, their mediations, and their histories to the notion of cosmopolitanism, I follow Neville Hoad's proviso for queer historiography: "it should not be possible to understand the initial theories of modern male homosexual identity in the west without looking at the imperial and neo-imperial contexts of such theoretical productions" (133). *Billy Budd* and *The Picture of Dorian Gray* both present examples of what Hoad has described as the "endlessly displaceable national and racial origins of homosexuality" (139).

In her groundbreaking study *The Epistemology of the Closet*, Eve Sedgwick famously classifies fictional works by Melville, Wilde, Marcel Proust, and Henry James as the "foundational texts of modern gay male identity." Attending to the binary play between the visible and invisible that undergirds her study, Sedgwick mentions the "international bond" among these texts (*Billy Budd* and *The Picture of Dorian Gray* in particular) as an important quality "efface[d]" by "canonic regimentation." However, Sedgwick treats the "international canvas" from which modern gay male identity emerges as a historical accident, symptomatically occluded by the requisite nationalism of canon formation in the humanities. I offer, alternatively, that same international canvas as itself a catalyst for newly mobile desires and newly eroticized encounters. The international flow of both fictional narratives and reader markets charts the field for a newly cathected sensibility since designated as "modern" and "gay."

Rather than taking for granted the coincidence of these two categories—"modern" and "gay"—I wish to consider what material conditions produce this conjunction. In part, I propose the figure of the primitive as an invisible component of the modern gay, reading the representations of Billy Budd and Dorian Gray as peculiar blond primitives and objects of disowned, racialized desire.

"Gay cosmopolitan" here designates a subject position beginning with (but not limited to) a white, urban, leisure-class gay male whose desire becomes globalized at the close of the nineteenth century. I hypothesize that the modern gay male identity often traced to sexology's late Victorian constructions of "invert" and "homosexual" occupies not the periphery of the nation but rather a cosmopolitan locus instrumental to colonial and neocolonial expansion. In her book *Terrorist Assemblages*, Jasbir Puar identifies "homonationalism" as the "successes of queer incorporation into the domains of consumer markets and social recognition in the post–civil rights, late twentieth-century" (xii). I also look to locate the homosexual in the life of the nation but argue that such analysis needs to begin not in the 1990s but perhaps in the 1890s or even earlier, with a reexamination of the emergence of a modern gay male identity and the scholarship on that emergence.[2] Rather than taking for granted the coincidence of "modern" and "gay," I inquire into what material conditions make this conjunction viable. I return to critical studies like Sedgwick's *Epistemology* and Michel Foucault's *History of Sexuality,* volume 1 (originally published in French in 1976) in order to reconsider the place of new mobilities (such as packaged travel) and new visual technologies (such as the cinema) vis-à-vis the birth of modern gay identity, traced to 1870 by Foucault and to 1891 by Sedgwick. (Of course, neither critic is interested in fixing a date, and these years are for each writer important historically yet to some degree arbitrary, the jumping off points for speculative genealogies more than indices of hard historicity.)

Taking as a starting point John D'Emilio's argument that capitalism creates conditions for a homosexual identity by staging (through wage labor) new spaces for socialization outside the family, I consider how homosexual desire circulates, not fortuitously but instrumentally, within the erotic economies of both capitalism and the nation. Rather than imagining the late Victorian invention of homosexuality singularly as a moment of abjection, I posit the homosexual as a modern agent of neocolonial expansion.

As a merchant mariner during wartime, Billy Budd occupies a markedly unstable position, neither civilian nor soldier, but something in between or in flux. With much of Melville's fiction, the ship is a site of cosmopolitan intercourse, peculiar for its extranational liminality and its constant literal navigation of/through national and international laws and domains. Merchant vessels, such as the one where we first encounter Billy, operate under a kind of mercenary nationalism, adopting what are known as "flags of convenience" in order to secure the most favorable economic conditions available within a world economy. (And it is in part this internationalism that Claire Denis seizes upon when she adapts Melville's seafaring story to the circumstance of French Foreign Legionnaires.) Yet, despite this fast and loose play with nationality and state allegiance (exacerbated by Billy's status as an orphan), Billy's ship is a part of the British merchant fleet, making it and its crew auxiliary subjects of the British naval force. Hence, Billy finds himself impressed for military service, removed from the English merchant vessel, the *Rights-of-Man*, and enlisted onto the man-of-war HMS *Bellipotent*. The names of the two ships, punctuated by Billy Budd's jovial bid farewell as he disembarks the merchant vessel, "And goodbye to you, too, old *Rights-of-Man*" (49), have, of course, invited endless allegorical interpretation, which I won't rehearse here other than to recall Thomas Paine's text of that title, the significance of its doctrine of inherent, natural rights to human rights discourse, hence, notions of global governance, and, within the narrative of Billy Budd, its gesture as well to the ideological and armed conflict between England and France. While Melville's choice of ship names is often read as a critique of the obliteration of human rights by martial law, we might also read the name of the merchant vessel as a reflection on the intercourse between rights discourse and commercialism, an especially prescient indictment in terms of the neoliberal course of mainstreamed gay liberation politics prevailing from the early 1990s to the present.

While the readings of Melville's allusion to Paine are numerous, I want to draw attention to the relatively neglected scene that opens the text, a peculiar tableau seemingly extraneous to the plot. Although the subtitle to *Billy Budd* promises an "inside narrative," the novella's perspective is hardly transparent, and in fact, the reader is as likely to pass over as to take note of the text's initial perspective, embedded in the first sentence of Melville's difficult prose, which is that of the "arrested" attention of a flaneur captivated by a "group of bronzed mariners . . . ashore on liberty." In fact, it is not the perspective of this apocryphal cruiser to which the reader is privy but rather that of the narrator, disavowed and projected onto the flaneur, strolling (or trolling) the docks. The sentence reads, "In a time before steamships, or then more frequently than now, a stroller along the docks of any considerable seaport would occasionally have his attention arrested by a group of bronzed mariners, man-of-war's men or merchant sailors in holiday attire, ashore on liberty." This hypothetical stroller conducts the narrator's disowned desire, then slips out of the narrative nearly imperceptibly.

This preliminary disavowal signals the text's own frustrated muteness, performatively embodied by Billy Budd's stutter. The rhetorical disavowal immediately throws into crisis the subtitle's promise of insider authority and authenticity. The inside narrative is hardly transparent or unmediated; rather, the text presents what Marty Roth has described as a "radically perplexed act of transmission."[3]

As the narrator moves from the perspective of the hypothetical flaneur to the narrator's own reverie of a "Handsome Sailor" flanked by lesser figures of his own class, we witness another curious deflection; rather than the blond, "welkin-eyed" Billy Budd, renamed "Beauty" or "Baby Budd" by his peers and memorialized in ballad, the narrator introduces the reader to "a common sailor so intensely black that he must needs have been a native African of the unadulterated blood of Ham—a symmetric figure much above the average height" (43). But this is no common sailor. In his very brief appearance in the tale, he is canonized as the sacred bull of sailors, first with an allusion to the constellation Taurus, within which the handsome sailor occupies the place of its brightest star, Aldebaran, and then through an analogy to the "grand sculptured Bull" to which Assyrian priests and faithful "prostrated themselves" (44).

According to the narrator's account, he encounters the African sailor in Liverpool, a cosmopolitan site of commerce as well as a crucial port for the slave trade. While the tributes to Billy Budd's beauty fix on his blond, pale whiteness in a way that registers another instance of the narrative's stuttered or muted transmissions, the description of the African sailor, the novella's proto-male "beauty," is elaborate and works also to establish a kind of cosmopolitan style and an erotic simultaneously manifested and sublimated:

> The two ends of a gay silk handkerchief thrown loose about the neck danced upon the displayed ebony of his chest, in his ears were big hoops of gold, and a Highland bonnet with a tartan band set off his shapely head. It was a hot noon in July; and his face, lustrous with perspiration, beamed with barbaric good humor. In jovial sallies right and left, his white teeth flashing into view, he rollicked along, the center of a company of his shipmates. These were made up of such an assortment of tribes and complexions as would have well fitted them to be marched up by Anacharsis Cloots before the bar of the first French Assembly of Representatives of the Human Race. (43)

Although the appearance of the African sailor in the tale is abbreviated to one short paragraph, I argue that Billy Budd serves as a proxy for the erotized exotic as much as the African sailor serves to mediate the narrative's muted and perplexed homoerotic desire. The exoticism embodied in the African sailor tempers with and through difference the dangerous sameness of the homosexual desire for which Billy becomes the object. If *Billy Budd* instances, as Sedgwick argues, the late-nineteenth-century emergence of a modern gay male identity, then it is critical also to interrogate the why and how of that conjunction between gay and modern. The march of the African sailor through Liverpool is fifty years removed from the telling of the story, and the narrator is also careful to locate his imagined flaneur in the "time before steamships." The narrative's effusive eroticization of Billy seems to require a further mediation across various nostalgic turns, whether the idealization of a preindustrial era, the fantasy of savage beauty joined to idyllic, dumb happiness in the figure of the African sailor whose face after all beams with "barbaric good humor," the contradictory fantasy of an unadulterated blackness (an untouched otherness) set in cosmopolitan Liverpool, or the persistent infantilization of Billy and its harkening for a pre-oedipal innocence, hence the epithet "Baby Budd." What work exactly does the adjective "modern" do in Sedgwick's formulation, "modern gay male"? What difference does modern make? To point to the obvious, the difference rests in modern's location of difference in temporality, specifically its nostalgic evocations of the child and the primitive as the pre-lives of gay male subjectivity. The question of the novella's "inside narrative" is then perhaps not so much a question of privileging the insider's authority as it is a question of the production of an inside itself and its constituent contradictory elements. The reader's task is less the determination of veracity (i.e., whose story most approximates actuality: the official military account, the sailors' lore recorded in the novella's concluding ballad, or the narrator's "radically perplexed act of transmission") than the appreciation of the emergence of a new kind of inside narrative and the determination of what outside violences (i.e., "imperial and neo-imperial contexts") are necessary for its claim to self-knowledge, a claim simultaneously to subjecthood and to self-transparency. As Neville Hoad explains, gay male identity, in its particularly "modern," late-nineteenth-century manifestation, requires evolutionary and primitivist logics in order to construct its "narrative of an ultimately unified *subject*, comprising a branching hierarchy in which the manifold others of this *subject* are perceived as already incorporated into and transcended by the *subject*. This incorporation and transcendence is achieved by the temporalisation of space" (133; emphasis his).

While scholarship on *Billy Budd* has neglected the African sailor introduced in the work's first page, twentieth-century writers and filmmakers such as Jean Genet, Rainer Werner Fassbinder, and Claire Denis have elaborated on the novella's Africanist presence. Genet's novel *Querelle* transforms the beautiful blond sailor into a figure closer to Wilde's Dorian Gray than to his original model, Billy Budd. Like Dorian, Querelle presents the murderous, cynical savage. Melville's African sailor is invoked in Genet's novel when Querelle appears to his enthralled admirer, Lieutenant Seblon, blackened by coal dust. Querelle, who has recently in the narrative discovered his pleasure in being "buggered" (by the brothel owner, Nono), uses the coal dust as a seductive veil—suggesting both the Africanist in *Billy Budd* and the Orientalism of *Dorian Gray*:

> The handsome blond boy, secretly adored, would very soon appear, naked perhaps, but re-invested with great majesty. The coal dust was not thick enough to quite conceal the brightness of the hair, the eyebrows and the skin, nor the rosy coloration of the lips and ears. It was obviously just a veil, and Querelle raised it now and again by occasionally, coquettishly, one might say artfully blowing on his arms or ruffling a curl of his hair. (85)

Querelle uses blackface as a means of playing with the norms of gender and sexuality that otherwise compel his behavior and that of the other male characters (sailors, laborers, policemen, and violent criminals) bound to class-specific standards of virility. His seduction of Seblon invokes both the blond beauty, Baby Budd, and the image of the exotic, ebony sailor. Querelle manipulates his "veil" of coal dust to create a racial masquerade:

> Well, certainly nothing but a little coal dust—familiar enough, in name and consistency; that simple ordinary stuff, so capable of making a face, a pair of hands, appear coarse and dirty—yet it invested this young blond

sailorboy with all the mysterious powers of a faun, of a heathen idol, of
a volcano, of a Melanesian archipelago. He was himself, yet he was so no
longer. (87)

Querelle's and Seblon's shared fantasies of blackness mediate the sail-
or's performance of a queered masculinity. The scene illustrates Hoad's
argument about the modern gay subject's "incorporation and transcendence" of the other "achieved through the temporalisation of space." The
working-class cosmopolitanism of sailors produces a geographic and
cultural knowledge through which that temporalization is elaborated
and authorized.

While Melville's *Billy Budd* offers a foundational text for modern gay
male identity, the endlessly perplexed transmissions of its inside narrative destabilize the construction of that identity as a unified subject,
but that destabilization can only be appreciated by attending to the significance of the narrator's nostalgia for the ebony sailor he encounters
on the docks of Liverpool. Genet's text (like Fassbinder's and Denis's
afterward) more fully deconstructs that unified subject. Melville's text,
after all, cannot deconstruct what it cannot name. But therein lies its
usefulness to Sedgwick's epistemology of the closet. However, I return
to this foundational gay text in order to reconsider the now taken-for-
granted centrality of the closet as the defining metaphor for modern
gay identity.

The privacy of the closet, of the epistemological and ontological
spaces demarcated as *inside*, depends upon the publicity of the brown
body—in this case, more specifically, an African body on the docks of
Liverpool "in the time before steamships"—but one that is reimagined
into a blond primitive. While Sedgwick attends to the production of
what she calls "nonce taxonomy"—the exemplary creative practice of
which she locates in the writing of Proust and James—I am concerned
with what might be termed the "nonce embodiments" that instead characterize *Billy Budd* as well as *The Picture of Dorian Gray*, the foundational works for her study.[4]

The contributions of *Epistemology of the Closet*, and for that matter Eve Sedgwick's entire body of work, are without a doubt groundbreaking and invaluable to cultural studies and literary scholarship on gender and sexuality. It is not my intent to undermine or depreciate these contributions. Much of the work I do would not be possible without the interventions of scholars like Sedgwick. In her famous "Axiomatic" introduction to *Epistemology of the Closet*, Sedgwick in fact anticipates and invites future contestations and revisions as a "measure of the success" of her analysis. The author cautions above all else against the categorical application of her analysis. In language that at moments recalls that of one of Melville's narrators, she explains,

> Any critical book makes endless choices of focus and methodology, and it is very difficult for these choices to be interpreted in any other light than that of the categorical imperative: the fact that they are made in a certain way here seems a priori to assert that they would be best made in the same way everywhere. I would ask that, however sweeping the claims made by this book may seem to be, it not be read as making that particular claim. Quite the opposite: a real measure of the success of such an analysis would lie in its ability, in the hands of an inquirer with different needs, talents, or positionings, to clarify the distinctive kinds of resistance offered to it from different spaces on the social map, even though such a project might require revisions or rupturings of the analysis as first proffered. The only imperative that the book means to treat as categorical is the very broad one of pursuing an antihomophobic inquiry. (14–15)

Sedgwick's requests appeal to the civility of the reader, rhetorically inoculating her argument from the kind of deconstructive analysis she outlines in the introduction. The choice of focus that prompts this edifying note is "the book's specification of male, and of Euro-American male, sexual definition as its subject" (13). My choice of the same subject, for significant portions of my own analysis, while in many ways made possible by Sedgwick, departs from her method of specification.

Sedgwick's defensive posture over her decision to specify a Euro-American male subject (in other words, her focus on canonical works of Western European and Anglo American literature) is I think misguided, belying—and making her complicit with—the ontological integrity granted a priori to that subject.

Following Foucault, her book traces an epistemic shift in sexual discourse:

> [I]n accord with Foucault's demonstration, whose results I will take to be axiomatic, that modern Western culture has placed what it calls sexuality in a more and more distinctively privileged relation to our most prized constructs of individual identity, truth, and knowledge, it becomes truer and truer that the language of sexuality not only intersects with but transforms the other languages and relations by which we know. (3)

What neither Sedgwick nor Foucault before her examines is the presumptive position of the Euro-American male as the subject of knowing and individual identity and how that very apriority may itself be contingent upon discourses of primitive or exotic sexuality. In other words, it is not only the figure of the African sailor tellingly absent from Sedgwick's analysis but also racial discourse more generally, including any discussion of the relation of whiteness to the emerging languages of sexuality. Sedgwick's use of the contraction "Euro-American" elides the transforming relations of whiteness to the emergent sexual discourse of the late nineteenth century but also the international course of that relation—the very dependence of this privileged sexual discourse on a cosmopolitan imagination. Hence, Sedgwick's omission of race as a construct pivotal to modernity's proliferation of sexual knowledge—of sexuality as knowledge—renders the book complicit with nationalist and imperialist projects.

To clarify, my objection is not to the focus on the Euro-American male but rather to the transparency he accrues as at once the specified subject of homo/heterosexual definition and the unspecified form of the subject as subject. The implications are profound if we keep in mind Sedgwick's contention that homo/heterosexual definition functions as a sort of "presiding master term" within a larger "cultural network of normative definitions" that includes, among other categories, knowledge/ignorance, private/public, masculine/feminine, and majority/minority. In order to privilege sexuality over other differences, Sedgwick appeals to a binary that could easily have been included in her list of oppositional schema, namely, visibility/invisibility. By reifying the distinction between what she designates as the visible (race) and the invisible (sexuality), Sedgwick treats race and sexuality as discrete rather than mutually constitutive operations. Hence the doubling in *Billy Budd* of the African sailor and the blond, welkin-eyed Baby Budd, figures that incite homoerotic desire but remain dumb (or uninitiated) to its circulation. The African sailor is both Billy's prototype and his twin; they are two and one. The emphatic publicity of the Handsome Sailor, of the "brown" (blond primitive) body, within the racial logics of white supremacy provides the counterpoint and foil to the closeted (private, urbane) sexuality of the Euro-American male subject.

As David Greven explains, Billy embodies a source of "homoerotic contagion," simultaneously binding and imperiling the homosocial utopia of Melville's shipboard: "he is a dangerous figure, a carrier of sexual intrigue who is himself sexually inert, empty, hollow, vacuous. He incites eroticism while he personally eradicates it."[5] As an agent of contagion, Billy Budd reproduces some version of himself in the sailors he infects. In the case of Claggart, he reproduces a dark twin. The master-at-arms projects his decadence into the hollow Billy (Greven's "blond nothingness"). As Greven explains, "one must see [Claggart's] knowledge of the 'bad' in Billy Budd as the postlapsarian knowledge of sex." Homo/heterosexual definition also reveals here the expression of nostalgia intrinsic to decadence. Claggart's repressed homosexual desire is the defining core of his decadence. His aggressions against Billy chart the disowned projections of that desire back to its source but also betray Claggart's resentment. The Handsome Sailor is the source of contagion, but he remains "inviolate." Billy's innocence is imagined as a childlike quality (i.e., "Baby Budd"). That childish quality is a metaphor for the idyllic epoch of the savage literalized in the figure of the African sailor on the docks of a preindustrial Liverpool. In Claggart (Sedgwick's prototype for the modern gay male), Melville constructs a figure beset by the decadence of proscribed sexuality confounded by a nostalgic desire to inhabit that sexuality innocently. Claggart's sexual modernity is conditioned on the temporal and spatial remoteness of a savage "brown" body.

Among her study's a priori conditions, the contradictions that escape Sedgwick's deconstructive analysis, is the opposition antihomosexual and prohomosexual. Sedgwick explains on the book's very first page that "[t]he contradictions I will be discussing are not in the first place those between prohomosexual and antihomosexual people or ideologies, although the book's strongest motivation is indeed the gay-affirmative one. Rather, the contradictions that seem most active are the ones internal to all the important twentieth-century understandings of homo/heterosexual definition, both heterosexist and antihomophobic" (1). In addition to locating pro- and antihomosexual ideologies oppositionally, the structure of Sedgwick's argument also situates the distinction between heterosexist and antihomophobic as, if not altogether a restatement of the first binary, at least then a parallel formulation. The meaning and power of the operations labeled either pro- or antihomosexual hardly correspond to the binary literalness suggested by their prefixes. They are subject to the same internal corrosiveness that Sedgwick charts within the litany of oppositional categories bound by the master term "homo/heterosexual definition." If homosexual and heterosexual are not discrete categories, then neither are pro- and antihomosexual. I would also argue that one can be antihomophobic without being homophilic and that Sedgwick's logic errs in aligning the gay-affirmative case with the antihomophobic one.

Melville provides his three primary characters with correspondent brown bodies. While Billy's correspondence to the figure of the African sailor—the original Handsome Sailor—is the most explicit, Claggart and Vere are also likened to exotic others, though less directly and persistently than Billy. Melville takes special care to attend in detail to Claggart's physiognomy. The description, consistent with the nineteenth-century science of phrenology, seeks to discern the signs of Claggart's deviance on his body.[6]

> His brow was of the sort phrenologically associated with more than average intellect; silken jet curls partly clustering over it, making a foil to the pallor below, a pallor tinged with a faint shade of amber akin to the hue of time-tinted marbles of old. This complexion, singularly contrasting with the red or deeply bronzed visages of the sailors, and in part the result of his official seclusion from the sunlight, though it was not exactly displeasing, nevertheless seemed to hint of something defective or abnormal in the constitution and blood. But his general aspect and manner were so suggestive of an education and career incongruous with his naval function that when not actively engaged in it he looked like a man of high quality, social and moral, who for reasons of his own was keeping incog. Nothing was known of his former life. It might be that he was an Englishman; and yet there lurked a bit of an accent in his speech suggesting that possibly he was not such by birth, but through naturalization in early childhood. (64–65)

Every detail of Claggart's anatomy suggests his deviance without ever naming it. The narrator confesses as much before beginning his description of the master-at-arms: "His portrait I essay, but shall never hit it" (64). Again the narrative's promise of "inside" authority is thwarted. Just as the master-at-arms remains "incog," the narrative protects Claggart's secret, which is the text's secret too.

As Tom McGlamery points out, the association of above-average intellect to sexual deviance is a common one in phrenology. Claggart's cultivated intellect is contrasted to the childlike innocence of Billy. Most queer readings understand Claggart's bitterly obsessive pursuit of Billy as an index of his frustrated same-sex desire for the handsome sailor.

But that desire may be more complicated than the lust for Billy's physique and youthful beauty attributed to Claggart. The master-at-arms may also covet Billy's innocence, an innocence akin to that of the African sailor who "beamed with barbaric good humor" in the narrator's elaborate reverie of a "less prosaic time." Billy too is described as a barbarian throughout the text. Claggart's yearning is sexual but also nostalgic; these two qualities of his desire may well be linked in the imagination of the gay cosmopolitan. In Billy Budd, Claggart locates the source of the homoerotic energies that circulate aboard the *Bellipotent* but also, for him, a disturbingly anachronous blond primitive: a figure that excites same-sex male desire yet remains innocent to its decadent corruption. Claggart's bitterness then is symptomatic of modernity's unspecified nostalgia. The master-at-arms' "high quality"—his obvious urbanity and refinement—leads to his downfall when matched against the imperviousness of Billy's primitive disposition. Claggart resents and longs for Billy's *un*-shamefulness.

Claggart's frustrated desire—a species of nostalgia—reverberates with the wistful reverie that frames the narrative. His marble-like pallor belongs decisively to the time since steamships. Before commencing his phrenological account of Claggart's features, the narrator glosses the history of the station of master-at-arms:

> Originally, doubtless, that petty officer's function was the instruction of the men in the use of arms, sword or cutlass. But very long ago, owing to the advance in gunnery making hand-to-hand encounters less frequent and giving to niter and sulphur the pre-eminence over steel, that function ceased; the master-at-arms of a great warship becoming a sort of chief of police charged among other matters with the duty of preserving order on the populous lower gun decks. (64)

Claggart is a distinctly modern creature compared to the bronzed sailors of whom Billy is a charmed specimen. If Billy binds the ship's homosocial utopia by inflaming desire between men, Claggart can only interrupt those circuits of desire through his policing. But Claggart's disruption of the homosocial utopia is not directly a function of his official station but rather the consequence of his status as harbinger of modernity's discontents: he is a bureaucrat among men. The narrator's phrenological diagnosis suggests an innate disorder, but the text complicates that reading by introducing the possibility that both narrator and master-at-arms share a telltale nostalgia for a time when men were men. Melville's text famously resolves very little, and it does not resolve whether Claggart's deviance results from nature or nurture (what Sedgwick would designate a contest between minoritizing versus universalizing readings). While the forehead and chin epitomize innate defect, the master-at-arms' hands, "too small and shapely to have been accustomed to toil" (64), indicate he is a victim of a more general cultural feminization, to which someone of his prominent class would be especially subject. His deviance then is located as much in his gender as it is in his sexuality, a still emergent field of knowledge at the time of the novella's composition.

While Billy's character is modeled on the "black pagod of a fellow" (43) who anticipates his arrival, Claggart's phrenology draws likewise on an exotic antecedent. The master-at-arms' chin, according to the narrator, is as "beardless as Tecumseh's" (64). Here gender deviance is racialized, and, since the issue of Claggart's abnormality remains unresolved (nature or nurture), so too Tecumseh becomes implicated retrospectively in the officer's sexual deviance. Unlike the many references to Billy as a barbarian, the comparison of Claggart to a Native American historical figure is both isolated and strangely specific. Why Tecumseh? The Shawnee leader commanded an Indian confederacy that allied with British forces against the United States during the War of 1812. The many factors leading to the conflict include accusations of British impressment of American sailors and British collaboration with American Indian resistance to United States territorial expansion. Typical of *Billy Budd*, the allusion is a provocative one that ultimately defies neat resolution.

The novella concludes with three conflicting accounts of Billy and Claggart's deaths: the official report of a naval chronicle published weekly, the unofficial oral history of a sailors' ballad, and the narrator's own account. Critics dispute the significance of these conflicting histories, which can serve either to authorize the narrator's story or alternately to destabilize any claim to the truth. While neither the official record of the naval chronicle nor the popular historical memory of the ballad seriously diminishes the authority of the narrator, his deflections (including the narrative's very first rhetorical gesture) suggest that his interest in the truth is neither unbiased nor transparent.

The unabashed bias of the other two accounts allow the narrator to situate himself as a balanced arbiter of the truth. They serve Melville's purpose well by introducing ironic play on the relationship between homosexual and the nation. The naval chronicle celebrates Claggart as one of a company of men on whose "efficiency . . . His Majesty's navy so largely depends." The reporter surmises that the "fidelity" of Claggart's service as a petty officer is "the greater because of his strong patriotic impulse." Within the context of the novella, this characterization ironically impugns the class to which Claggart belongs. The paragraph concludes, "In this instance as in so many other instances in these days the character of this unfortunate man signally refutes, if refutation were needed, that peevish saying attributed to the late Dr. Johnson, that patriotism is the last refuge of a scoundrel" (130).

As Thomas Scorza argues, Melville repeats in *Billy Budd* techniques he developed in earlier works such as *Typee*, *Omoo*, and *Redburn* that cleverly differentiate narrator from author.[7] Scorza reads the narrator's references to "an honest scholar, my senior" and "a writer whom few know" as creative devices by which Melville slyly inserts himself into the text as a primary yet oblique authority. Such moments register the circumlocutory course by which both narrator and author arrive at the privileged yet remote space of knowledge designated in the novella's parenthetical subtitle as the "inside," a space epistemologically privileged precisely for its remoteness. Scorza distinguishes between those critics who read *Billy Budd* as a historical novel (i.e., a "thinly veiled" account of the *Somers* mutiny of 1842) and those who present an entirely ironist reading of the work.[8] In both cases, he contends, critics settle the tension between author and narrator too expeditiously, eradicating it in the first case and rigidifying it in the latter. Any interpretation that definitively arrives at the text's inner truth necessarily simplifies the epistemological and moral imperatives of the novella as well as of Melville's larger oeuvre. For Scorza, the tension between author and narrator that characterizes much of Melville's writing dramatizes the dilemmas of witnessing, in particular the impossibility of condensing into one historical record the fullness and complexity of human life. Melville achieves with this tension "a different kind of writing altogether" (Scorza 8); the resulting ambiguities productively memorialize and—through a dialogic engagement with the reader—write the gaps in the historical record, without substituting one definitive authority for another. As Scorza expains,

> What the narrator presents as a contrast between the historically accurate and the historically inaccurate is actually the author's means of approaching a truth which is beyond the purview of historical writing. The narrator's internal lesson, that a historical record of events does not reveal the truth, must be applied by the critic to Melville's creation, *Billy Budd, Sailor*, as a whole. (8)

I concur with Scorza and like-minded critics who argue in favor of plumbing the contradictions and tensions of the narrative rather than insisting on a resolution to its problems. At the same time, I wonder too if Scorza's assessment of Melville's epistemological project in *Billy Budd* is not ultimately itself too tidy. This is not to say that I disagree with his conclusion, only that I think there is also more to it. Critics such as Barbara Johnson, Eve Sedgwick, and David Greven, like Scorza, understand the paradoxical qualities of the text as a kind of epistemological treatise undertaken by Melville, but they link the narrative's more abstract questions about the nature of knowledge to questions about self-knowledge and sexuality. Hence, for Sedgwick, *Billy Budd* stands as foundational text documenting both the emergence of a male homosexual identity and the epistemology of the gay closet. In fact, the two constructs (homosexual and closet) are coterminous. *Billy Budd* as a foundational gay text not only documents the closet; it performs it.

The subtitle of the novella promises the authenticity of "inside" knowledge. Ultimately, the narrative establishes the parameters of that "inside" through indirection and negation. The reader is left to surmise the contents of a privileged location of truth that remains nonetheless inviolable. Sedgwick focuses primarily on Claggart as the originary model for the repressed homosexual, a figure of unspeakable knowledge that designates the text's construction of psychological interiority, the subject's vexed (even occluded) access to that interiority, and the symptomatic nature of that thwarted and disavowed self-knowledge. Her attention to Claggart, however, neglects the circumlocutions and indirections of the narrative that arguably also enact the text's closetedness. Even the parentheses that enclose the subtitle foreclose grammatically the rarefied space of the narrative's promised interiority. The "Inside Narrative" is contained, secret-*ed* within punctuation that ideographically replicates the architecture of the closet. What concerns me most here is the relationship between the primitive and the construction of interiority. The African sailor is necessary to establish Billy Budd as blond primitive (both are described as barbarian), and the vacuity of Billy Budd is necessary to construct the interiority of the repressed homosexual, Claggart. The eroticized figure of the Handsome Sailor functions both to inspire homosexual desire and to complete a dichotomy between primitive and urbane constitutive of the modern gay male's very modernity.

As Greven points out, critical interpretation of *Billy Budd* has largely neglected the title character in favor of analyses of Claggart and Captain Vere. Greven argues persuasively that Billy Budd, "constructed as a sexually inviolate and unavailable male, incites male utopia" aboard the *Bellipotent*. More importantly for Greven, the all-male utopian scene of the ship is "one both facilitated and endangered by the new Handsome Sailor." Remarkably, Greven returns to the text's first paragraph, emphasizing the significance of even the first sentence in crafting the novella's homosocial world, yet he suppresses the specifically African and cosmopolitan identity of the text's original Handsome Sailor:

> The Handsome Sailor is not a person, but a looming and monolithic fantasy, a "signal object" around which the men—all the men in the world, since these men represent the human race—revolve like satellites. . . . From the story's start, the male world of *Billy Budd* hinges on the trope of male beauty, an attribute apotheosized into an ideal.

Billy's good humor remains unchanged as he faces execution. The description of Billy's innocence links the narrative's atavism and nostalgia to the queer desire for the Handsome Sailor's body. Billy's youth contributes to his beauty, but the narrator also associates youthful innocence with a cherished fantasy of "barbarian" life before Christian contact, whether that be the inhabitants of the British Isles before the Roman invasion or contemporaneous "savages" removed to London.

> Not that like children Billy was incapable of conceiving what death really is. No, but he was wholly without irrational fear of it, a fear more prevalent in highly civilized communities than those so-called barbarous ones which in all respects stand nearer to unadulterated Nature. And, as elsewhere said, a barbarian Billy radically was—as much so, for all the costume, as his countrymen the British captives, living trophies, made to march in the Roman triumph of Germanicus. Quite as much so as those later barbarians, young men probably, and picked specimens among the earlier British converts to Christianity, at least nominally such, taken to Rome (as today converts from lesser isles of the sea may be taken to London), of whom the Pope of that time, admiring the strangeness of their personal beauty so unlike the Italian stamp, their clear ruddy complexion and curled flaxen locks, exclaimed "Angles" (meaning *English*, the modern derivative), "Angles, do you call them? And is it because they look so like angels?" Had it been later in time, one would think that the Pope had

in mind Fra Angelico's seraphs, some of whom, plucking apples in the gardens of the Hesperides, have the faint rosebud complexion of the more beautiful English girls. (120–21)

The narrator transforms Billy the child into Billy the barbarian. Baby Budd's childlike qualities function to translate the narrative's nostalgia for a fantasied erotic primitivism. In a striking reversal, it is the "highly civilized" sensibility that ultimately proves irrational. If Billy is crude intellectually, he is also closer to "unadulterated Nature." The decadence of Claggart (or the narrator—since it is his fantasy of Billy to which we are most directly privy) represents then not a corruption of social norms but rather the alienation of civilized man from nature. Even more striking is the othering of blondness: the rosy complexion and yellow hair of idealized Western beauty exoticized, made strange. Almost as quickly as the British barbarians, beautiful young men, arrive in Rome and are presented to the pope does the description leap both forward and backward to Fra Angelico in the fifteenth century and to the pagan image of the Hesperides, whose orchards produce not the deadly fruit of the book of Genesis but rather golden apples of immortality. Much like the opening sentence of the novella, the sudden—if brief—transition to a second person (in this instance, the pope) dissociates the narrator from his own homoerotic reverie. In yet a further imaginative dissociation, the barbarians ("young men probably") transform into "beautiful English girls."

The reversal of the privileged position in the binary civilized/barbaric supports Sedgwick's reading of an earlier passage where the narrator concludes that for one such as Claggart, "the mania of an evil nature, not engendered by vicious training or corrupting books or licentious living, [is] but born with him and innate, in short 'a depravity according to nature'" (76). The narrator quotes from Plato's tautological definition for "Natural Depravity." As Sedgwick explains, however,

The narrative does not pause to remark . . . that the platonic "definition" is worse than tautological, suggesting as it does two diametrically opposite meanings. "A depravity according to nature," like "natural depravity," might denote something that is depraved when measured against the external standard of nature—that is, something whose depravity is unnatural. Either of the same two phrases might also denote, however, something whose proper nature it is to be depraved—that is, something whose depravity is natural. So all the definition accomplishes here is to carry the damning ethical sanctions already accumulated into a new semantic field, that of nature and the *contra naturam*—a field already entangled for centuries with proto-forms of the struggles around homosexual definition. (95)

The classification of "natural depravity" introduced by the narrator in his diagnosis of the master-at-arms does not so much isolate the condition of Claggart's decadence as embroil the narrator in its very obfuscation, making him party to a kind of rhetorical perversion where oppositional binaries are rendered transposable. It also situates his discourse, as Sedgwick insightfully observes, at the crux of the problem of homosexual definition.

Arguably, it is not Claggart's homosexual desire that corrupts him but rather his repression of that desire. The narrator warns the reader against confusing the platonic definition of natural depravity with the Calvinist dogma it may recall. Here Melville would seem to invoke the notion of repression common to both an emerging pathologized understanding of homosexuality and the minoritarian politic it engenders: "Civilization, especially if of the austerer sort, is auspicious to it" (75).

Curiously, both Billy and Claggart are cast as foreign. In both cases, their differences are located in speech, Claggart's accented, Billy's stammering. As with the orphaned Billy, "nothing was known of [Claggart's] former life" (64–65). Rumors aboard the *Bellipotent* impugn Claggart as both a foreigner and a swindler.[9] The hint of an accent in his speech leads to the speculation that if he is indeed an Englishman, he "was not such by birth, but through naturalization in early childhood" (65). As he is an orphan, Billy's origins also remain mysterious. Not only is he repeatedly likened to a barbarian; his stutter rehearses the etymology of the very word, which is derived from a Greek word meaning "foreign" or "not-Greek," the repetition of the first two syllables ("bar-bar") mocking the supposed stammering of a foreign and uncivilized tongue. One might argue that Claggart's depravity—his evil mania—results from civilization's proscription of homoerotic desires, while Billy represents the nostalgic return to a pure state in nature, a condition prior to gay shame. If the unified subject of modern gay identity, as Hoad argues, requires the incorporation and transcendence of an other, that subject, in the figure of Claggart, comes undone when confronted with Billy Budd, a projected version of the other not only radically temporalized as child/barbarian but also sexually inviolate. It's not just that Claggart can't have Billy, as most critics suggest; it's also that Claggart can neither be nor assimilate him. It's always too late for that "austerer sort" to forget his shame and return to a state of "unadulterated Nature."

The ship chaplain's last rites for Billy read more like an unsuccessful attempt to convert a savage:[10]

> If in vain the good chaplain sought to impress the young barbarian with ideas of death akin to those conveyed in the skull, dial, and crossbones on old tombstones, equally futile to all appearance were his efforts to bring home to him the thought of salvation and a Savior. Billy listened, but less out of awe or reverence, perhaps, than from a certain natural politeness, doubtless at bottom regarding all that in much the same way that most mariners of his class take any discourse abstract or out of the common tone of the workaday world. And this sailor way of taking clerical discourse is not wholly unlike the way in which the primer of Christianity, full of transcendent miracles, was received long ago on tropic isles by any superior *savage*, so called—a Tahitian, say of Captain Cook's time or shortly after that time. (121)

Again, the narrative not only seeks barbarian and savage complements for Billy but also endlessly displaces Billy's engagement with the text's modern gay subjects (Claggart, Vere, the narrator, the reader?) back-ward across time. The narrator's various fantasies of cosmopolitan first encounter—the stroller and the African sailor in Liverpool, the pope and the ruddy-complexioned British captives, Captain Cook and a Tahitian—nostalgically convey the modern gay male subject to what is imagined as a time and space of unconstrained eroticism.

2

"Going to Meet the Man" in Abu Ghraib

The notion of secrecy is central to James Baldwin's short story "Going to Meet the Man," not only thematically but also formally, as the tableau of one embedded secret memory successively opens onto that of another. The narrative never explicitly names its secret, because it remains illegible to the story's narrative consciousness, that of the protagonist, Jesse, a white deputy sheriff in the Jim Crow South. What is made plain in the story is that this secret consolidates Jesse's community of white supremacists. Baldwin represents whiteness as a kind of ontological closet, if I may riff on Eve Sedgwick's famous formulation.

I am struck also by how the narrative's structuring secret seemingly has infected readers historically. The dearth of critical attention paid to this story becomes that much more conspicuous in comparison, say, to the body of scholarship attending to "Sonny's Blues," published in 1965, in the same collection for which "Going to Meet the Man," after all, provides the title story.[1]

It should be clear from my title, "'Going to Meet the Man' in Abu Ghraib," that I look to Baldwin's story for analytical tools that might be applied to understanding the nature of the photographs that emerged following news of the abuses, including torture and murder, occurring at the Abu Ghraib prison in Iraq. The analogy to the culture of lynching was immediate to me as it was to many spectators. Following the publication of the photos, writer and art historian Luc Sante, in a *New York Times* op-ed piece, registered the uncanny evocation by the Abu Ghraib photos of the archive of lynching postcards:

The first shot I saw, of Specialist Charles A. Graner and Pfc. Lynndie R. England flashing thumbs up behind a pile of their naked victims, was so jarring that for a few seconds I took it for a montage. When I registered what I was seeing, I was reminded of something. There was something familiar about that jaunty insouciance, that unabashed triumph at having inflicted misery upon other humans. And then I remembered: the last time I had seen that conjunction of elements was in photographs of lynchings.[2]

Most critically here, what jars Sante's memory is less the dehumanized images of the Iraqis than the shameless expressions on the faces of the U.S. soldiers: "Often the spectators at lynchings of African-Americans are so effusive in their mugging that they all seem to be vying for credit. Before seeing such pictures you might expect the faces in them to express some kind of collective rage; instead the mood is giddy, often verging on hysterical, with a distinct sexual undercurrent."

Certainly, Sante's description of these faces recalls Baldwin's fictionalization of the experience of white spectator-participants at a lynching in "Going to Meet the Man." If the narrative's structuring secret remains illegible to the protagonist, its "distinct sexual undercurrent" is less of a secret to the reader. I extend Baldwin's reading of this race secret to the abuses that occurred at the Abu Ghraib military prison in order not only to better understand the racialized and sexual nature of the violence but also to determine what about it was symptomatically American. I ask how the race secret in this instance is cast violently onto the globe. While I do think it is instructive and relevant to read lynching photography and culture next to Abu Ghraib's torture archive, I remain cautious about the use of analogy as a critical practice and its own potential violences. An analogy between the culture of lynching and Abu Ghraib risks serious erasure. The domestic history of U.S. racist violence is always threatened by the aggressive amnesia of the nation. With respect to the photographic texts from Abu Ghraib, the analogy to lynching risks inordinately domesticating the specificities of its colonial violence. Analogy, in this sense, risks collusion with the imperial project. Jasbir Puar, among others, reports the

Orientalist fantasies at work in the Bush administration's war machine and how those fantasies infused its operations on the ground, including prison abuses at Abu Ghraib. A too-simple analogy to the culture of lynching erases what Puar understands as an assemblage of imperial histories that come together to create the Muslim body as an object of torture. Puar documents, for instance, how the U.S. "knowledge" of the Muslim body is also drawn from "Israeli surveillance and occupation measures . . . the behavior of the French in Algeria, and even the 2002 Gujarat pogrom in India—[which] surge together to create the Muslim body as a particular typological object of torture."[3] I do not want to diminish the particularity of either site: the lynching of black bodies in the United States or the torture of Iraqi bodies at Abu Ghraib. However, I do think it crucial to study how the stories of these particularities may be multiply and profoundly imbricated, especially where that imbrication is at once conspicuous and disarticulated. I pursue this difficulty through the prism of a homoerotic racialism. The Abu Ghraib photos drew immediate criticism for their homophobia, but lost in that criticism was the obvious homoeroticism of the photos. The problem is in part a hermeneutical one presented by the peculiar but hardly uncommon conjunction of homoerotics and U.S. empire: what is the relation between the homoerotics of racist violence and modern gay identity? In other words, my emphasis here is on locating continuities rather than analogies. Hazel Carby stresses the importance of not neglecting such continuities: "The importance of spectacles of abuse, the taking of photographs and videos, the preservation and the *circulation* of the visual image of the tortured/lynched body, the erotic sexual exploitation which produced pleasure in the torturers—all these practices are *continuities* in the history of American racism."[4] Nonetheless, finding these continuities inevitably puts into play any number of analogies; hence, the need to establish some caveats:

1. Any such continuity (or analogy) needs to be read against a teleological impulse; in other words, rather than turning to a domestic

history of racist violence to which we can append Abu Ghraib, we might also consider what we learn about the culture of lynching in Abu Ghraib (as I suggest with the title of this chapter).

2. We need to resist the tendency of analogy to rigidify the elements of its comparison even as it purportedly destabilizes them ontologically; for instance, the analogy between lynching and Abu Ghraib risks reifying as domestic the violence of lynching and reifying as international the violence of prison torture. It would be more instructive to ask how the culture of lynching may be linked also to histories of U.S. imperialism and how, obviously, the prisoner abuse at Abu Ghraib needs also to be understood within a history of the prison industrial complex that is both domestic and international.

3. The analogy creates a tendency toward a kind of analytic tidiness that forecloses other histories; here I would point to Colin Dayan's book on the history of the notion of "cruel and unusual punishment," where she locates preconditions that made Abu Ghraib possible in antebellum legislation that recognized the rights of slaves while simultaneously dehumanizing them.[5]

4. Analogies risk reproducing and further entrenching silences. As I discuss in my close reading of the story, Baldwin's privileging of the castrated black male body as *the* emblem of racist violence in the United States is complicit in silencing the sanctioned rape of black women. Likewise, the most publicized images of torture at Abu Ghraib foreground the bodies of white U.S. soldiers, both male and female, and of Iraqi prisoners, male only, while photos of female prisoners at Abu Ghraib, raped and subjected to sexual humiliations no less horrific than that of their male counterparts, have effectively been suppressed, not only by the state but also by its critics. Furthermore, gender analysis has focused almost exclusively on the problematic media representations of white women soldiers following the break of the story. But here also it is useful to insist on continuity rather than analogy. How might Baldwin's

story aid us in understanding these rippling silences? If we consider together the erasure of violence against women particular to both scenes, what alternative histories of the imbrication of race, sexuality, gender, and nation might be suggested?

James Baldwin's "Going to Meet the Man" traces queer desires profoundly rooted in American formations of white masculinity. I argue in this chapter that dominant white masculinity—which may include various U.S. institutionalizations such as Jim Crow, U.S. military culture, and neocolonialism—never perfectly aligns with heterosexuality, and in fact foments at its emergence a racial indivisibility that transcends sexual identifications. Baldwin rewrites the oedipal complex in his short story in order to locate a violent homoerotic interracialism as the foundation of sexual modernity and shared trait of white colonial masculinity—both homosexual and heterosexual.[6] However, he does not universalize a single model for the oedipal family romance, providing instead a primal scene for a specifically U.S.-centered, raced sexual embodiment. More significantly, Baldwin's primal scene determines a fundamental white desire consistent across "positive" (heterosexual) and "negative" (homosexual) resolutions of the oedipal phase.

The story, set during the civil rights era, begins with Jesse, a southern white deputy sheriff, trying unsuccessfully to achieve an erection, lying in bed next to the "frail sanctuary of his wife" Grace: "Excitement filled him like a toothache, but it refused to enter his flesh."[7] Jesse's excitement remains so long as he banishes from his imagination its primal object: the black man's body, or more precisely the black man's dick and all its mythic capacity. For Baldwin, the black woman's body approximates the object of desire but falls short: "The image of a black girl caused a distant excitement in him, like a far away light; but, again, the excitement was more like pain; instead of forcing him to act, it made action impossible" (229). The black woman's body as it is imagined by white dominant culture not only actively establishes Grace's body as the "frail sanctuary" (229) but also authorizes Jesse's rape of black women.

Sometimes, sure, like any other man, he knew that he wanted a little more spice than Grace could give him and he would drive over yonder and pick up a black piece or arrest her, it came to the same thing, but he couldn't do that now, no more. *There was no telling what might happen once your ass was in the air.* And they were low enough to kill a man then, too, every one of them, or the girl herself might do it. (230; emphasis mine)

For Jesse, the rape of a black woman is a legal impossibility. Just as the black man is reduced to his, she is reduced to her "black piece." Black women are to Jesse a kind of property that he reclaims at his whim; law enforcement in the United States functions as an extension of slavery. What Baldwin records in Jesse's rumination is the persistence of the institutionalized rape of black women: "pick[ing] up a black piece" is newly designated, after manumission, as "arrest." Jesse's image of his own "ass up in the air" metonymically represents his susceptibility to violent retribution while also connoting his own vulnerability to black penetration even while he rapes black women. Jesse's choice of this image foreshadows the revelations to come at the story's conclusion regarding the sexual fantasies he must keep secret even from himself and, for the purposes of Baldwin's psycho-social analysis of the racial secret, divulges the homoerotic racialism of white male community— and in a white supremacist and patriarchal culture, by extension, the nation. When Jesse worries, "There was no telling what might happen when you had your ass up in the air," he expresses at once his manifest sense of vulnerability to retributive black male violence and a latent desire for that violence to take the form of anal rape.

Jesse's attempts to achieve an erection lead him to thinking about the black women he raped, abusing his authority as a deputy sheriff. Succumbing temporarily to his impotence, Jesse turns toward Grace, whose "frail sanctuary" of a body replicates the sanctuary of his mother's womb: "He felt that he would like to hold her, hold her, hold her, and be buried in her like a child and never have to get up in the morning again and go downtown to face those faces, good Christ, they were ugly!" (230). Jesse's regression is motivated not only by the work day ahead of him, during which he will be likely to violently confront black civil rights protesters, but also by his impotence. He regresses both to avoid getting up and to forget not getting it up. What he can't escape is the link between the two: the brutalized black body and his own sexual excitement. His regression eventually returns him to his oedipal phase, but first he revisits the events of the previous day. This musing over the day's events is not a chance recollection but very much connected to his impotence. Ordered to stop the singing by civil rights protesters, Jesse realizes that he does not command the authority to accomplish this task and decides instead to make their "ring leader," already imprisoned and brutally beaten, stop the singing: "I couldn't make them stop for me but I knew he could make them stop" (232). Because the "ring leader" is in jail precisely for not submitting to the demands of law enforcement, it seems unlikely that Jesse can really expect him to do so now. The black man "lying on the ground jerking and moaning . . . and blood . . . coming out his ears" (232) provides Jesse with an opportunity to recover his mascu-linity, diminished by growing black resistance as well by the presence of his immediate superior, the sheriff, "Big Jim C." The "ring leader" has already been whipped by "Big Jim C. and his boys," and Jesse's contest with the black man is also a contest with Big Jim C. The typical oedipal triangulation is disrupted by the presence of the black man. The oedipal complex easily accommodates the figure of Grace, already established as both mother and love object, as well as the aptly named "Big Jim C," the "C" an injunction to look, to "see" how big Jim really is, Jesse once again subjected to the threat of the father's phallus. This disruption, as we find out later in the story, repeats symbolically that of his original oedipal crisis.

Ferociously beaten, the "ring leader" nonetheless possesses a sym-bolic authority that is insurmountable to the imaginations of both Jesse and his immediate superior, the sheriff, "Big Jim C." The sheriff is the first to imbue the black man with the authority he lacks. Jesse describes to Grace the police intimidation of blacks attempting to register to vote:

They had this line you know, to register . . . and they wouldn't stay where
Big Jim C. wanted them, no, they had to start blocking traffic all around
the court house so couldn't nothing or nobody get through, and Big Jim
C. figured that the others would move if this nigger would move, him being the ring leader, but he wouldn't move and he wouldn't let the others
move, so they had to beat him and a couple of the others and they threw
them in the wagon. . . . (232)

Like Big Jim C. before him, Jesse tries to recuperate the power he
believes he has forfeited to the black man but inadvertently assigns him
even greater authority symbolically. He begins by assuming his own
helplessness in the face of the defiant black singing and determines that
the "ring leader," who remains unnamed in the story—securing his status as both symbol and fantasy, incapacitated and nearly mute as a result
of the prior beating at the hands of Big Jim C. and his boys—possesses
the power that he lacks. Jesse compensates by using a cattle prod to further torture the black man. He requires the cattle prod if he is to be
properly equipped for this contest with the black man who once again,
as with Melville's African sailor, is described as a (sacred) bull, a "goddamn bull" (233).

The cattle prod approximates for Jesse then the mythic manhood he
has attributed to black men: "I put the prod to him and he jerked some
more and he kind of screamed—but he didn't have much voice left. . . .
I put it to him again, under his arms, and he just rolled around on the
floor and blood started coming from his mouth. He'd pissed his pants
already." Here Jesse pauses. "His mouth felt dry and his throat was as
rough as sandpaper; as he talked, he began to hurt all over with that
peculiar excitement which refused to be released" (232). Violently humiliating the black man with the prod excites Jesse sexually. His assault
becomes increasingly sexual: "he kept prodding the boy, sweat pouring
from beneath the helmet he had not yet taken off. The boy rolled around
in his own dirt and water and blood and tried to scream again as the

prod hit his testicles, but the scream did not come out, only a kind of rattle and a moan" (233).

The excitement Jesse experiences from assaulting his black prisoner summons an earlier, similar scene, although he cannot immediately reconstruct that memory: "he felt very close to a very peculiar, particular joy; something deep in him and deep in his memory was stirred, but whatever was in his memory eluded him" (233). The consciousness of that memory is interrupted by the prisoner's voice when he calls to Jesse from the floor, "White man . . . You remember Old Julia?" (233). However, the black man's voice and his aggressive hailing of Jesse as "white man" function simultaneously to return Jesse to that deeply repressed scene that he has unwittingly reenacted. Although the memory still eludes him, it reignites affects that lie deep inside. Jesse protects himself from retributive castration: "For some reason, he grabbed his privates" (233). He has not yet fixed the events that might correspond to the affects now ruling his body, although the infantile euphemism for genitals suggests a childhood memory. The prisoner's question temporarily distracts him. He remembers his first encounter with his prisoner, who had as a child similarly, and boldly, hailed him by the words "white man," responding impudently to Jesse's offer of chewing gum: "I don't want nothing you got, white man" (234)—the black child's rejoinder also a defense against the putative rationale for the lynching that concludes the story. Having now identified his prisoner as that same little boy, Jesse is filled with rage. He screams, "You lucky we pump some white blood into you every once in a while—your women! Here's what I got for all the black bitches in the world—!" (235). Baldwin describes the actions that accompany Jesse's invective. "Then he was, abruptly, almost too weak to stand; to his bewilderment, his horror, beneath his own fingers, he felt himself violently stiffen—with no warning at all; he dropped his hands and he stared at the boy and he left the cell" (235). Jesse's excitement results again from the sexually charged confrontation with the black man. Although as the beneficiary of Jesse's "white blood," the pronoun "you" most obviously would seem to designate the black race in general, Jesse's anxious clarification, "—your women," suggests that he in fact might be thinking of pumping black men, instead of or at least in addition to black women. It is this realization of homosexual desire that rouses his bewilderment and horror.

A series of associations—the black voices he is powerless to stop; the jailhouse beating; his impotence with Grace—transport Jesse back to a primal scene. He is filled both with "overwhelming fear" and "a curious and dreadful pleasure" (239). His recollection finds him initially seated in a car between his father and mother, his head resting on his mother's lap. Unlike his current circumstance with Grace, the young Jesse feels "sleepy . . . yet full of excitement" (239). Up until this point, Baldwin has used the word "excitement" in the story exclusively to indicate sexual stimulation, leading the reader to understand his youthful excitement here also as sexual—a result of his physical proximity to both his mother and father, especially as he intercepts the sexual energy between them. A black spiritual links the civil rights unrest and Jesse's police brutality to a lynching from his childhood. The erotic play and innuendo between Jesse's father and mother is mediated by the culture of lynching that now also entangles the boy:

> "I guess they singing for him," his father said, seeming very weary and subdued now. "Even when they're sad, they sound like they just about to go and tear off a piece." He yawned and leaned across the boy and slapped his wife lightly on the shoulder, allowing his hand to rest there for a moment. "Don't they?"
>
> "Don't talk that way," she said.
>
> "Well, that's what we going to do," he said, "you can make up your mind to that." He started whistling. "You see? When I begin to feel it, I gets kind of musical, too." (239–40)

In the midst (literally) of his parents' flirting, Jesse thinks of his black friend Otis, although he does not know why. His immediate memory is of wrestling with Otis in the dirt.[8] That night, which turns out to be the eve of the first lynching he witnesses, Jesse overhears his parents having sex. The black spirituals function as a chorus to Jesse's sexual initiation, now necessarily inflected by the culture of lynching with all its attendant sexual violence and fantasy. The next morning men and women rush to include Jesse's family in the news of the lynching. The women arrive, "some flushed and some pale with excitement." Jesse notices "everyone looking excited and shining" (241) as they congregate in preparation for the feast and communion that also comprise the ritual of lynching. With Jesse's observation, that the activities recall a Fourth of July picnic (242), Baldwin situates racial-sexual violence at the foundations of American freedom.

Jesse's mother makes herself pretty for the lynching, choosing her best dress and putting ribbons in her hair; she wears in fact the same dress she wears to church, again marking the lynching as a kind of communion. As the family arrives at the site of the lynching, the mother checks her appearance in the car mirror. The black man who will be lynched, now in sight of Jesse's father, is explicitly identified as part of an erotic triangulation between the husband and wife. "'You look all right,' said the father, and laughed. 'When that nigger looks at you, he's going to swear he threw his life away for nothing. Wouldn't be surprised if he don't come back to haunt you'" (244). The words are prophetic, since the black man indeed will lose his life for nothing; no crime was committed. And he—or more precisely, the black man symbolically—will continue to haunt Jesse, his parents, and white identity. His father's repeated laughter also marks the triangulation of the sexual relationship; the first voice Jesse notes when he overhears his parents having sex is "his father's voice in the other room, low, with a joke in it" (241). The laughter registers the murderousness of desire, and it actuates its own dissimulation by the interleaf of aggression with pleasure. Laughter's baring of teeth symbolizes the cannibalistic identifications of white masculinity. Jesse's father quite literally licks his chops at the sight of the lynched black man, still blocked from Jesse's view by other adult bodies:

They were looking at something he could not see. His lips had a strange, cruel curve, he wet his lips from time to time, and swallowed. He was terribly aware of his father's tongue, it was as though he had never seen it before. And his father's body suddenly seemed immense, bigger than a mountain. His eyes, which were grey green, looked yellow in the sunlight; or at least there was a light in them which he had never seen before.[9] (244)

The black male body disrupts the conventional family romance. Not only do Jesse's mother and father variously enact their desire for the black man, but every articulation of their desire for one another is mediated by the black man's body. However Jesse should resolve his oedipal complex, the desire for the black male body persists. The parents' mutual desire for the black man confounds the child's identifications. If Jesse resolves his oedipal complex positively, then he necessarily identifies not only with his father but also with the black man (who now also stands as the object of his mother's desire). Either oedipal resolution in fact results in Jesse's desire to be and to have the black male body. The negative resolution, whereby the male child identifies with his mother, situates the black man as the object of Jesse's desire; but this resolution also motivates an identification with the black man, who is likewise desired by the father. So that he might witness the black man's castration, his father lifts Jesse onto his shoulders, producing even more erotic and identificatory possibilities for the child. Jesse's station on his father's shoulders complicates the male child's castration anxiety. Legs straddled around his father's neck, his position suggests his vulnerability to castration by the father—who, because of the proximity of their flesh, can detect Jesse's excitement or lack thereof—as well as suggesting the father's vulnerability to castration symbolically by decapitation.[10] Finally laying eyes on the lynched body, Jesse focuses on the black man's head, for which he immediately substitutes his father's head: "He saw the forehead, flat and high, with a kind of arrow of hair in the center, like he had, like his father had; they called it a widow's peak" (246). This substitution seemingly satisfies his need to eliminate his father as competitor for his mother's affection, the hanging (castrate) head indicating her presence now as widow. The father's head, isolated between the forfex of Jesse's legs, risks decapitation. The widow's peak marks Jesse's patricidal desire. However, from his vantage point, Jesse recognizes between his legs the insignia of his own vulnerability, as he too shares the widow's peak. As Jesse's eyes wander over the man's body, the black man begins to more emphatically displace the father and disrupt the family romance. Jesse notes that "he was a big man, a bigger man than his father, and black as an African jungle Cat, and naked" (246). Nonetheless, Jesse's imagination has now incorporated the black male figure as "a big man, a bigger man than his father." The urgency with which he dehumanizes the black man as an "African jungle Cat" and exploits his humiliating nakedness only serves to underscores Jesse's intensifying anxiety. Alarmed by the man's agonized scream when the flames reach his body, "Jesse clung to his father's neck in terror as the cry rolled over the crowd" (246). Jesse's conflicted desires for the black man comprise the race secret of whiteness. He realizes that his people share a secret but can never articulate that secret nor inquire into its nature: "*What did he do?* Jesse wondered. *What did the man do? What did he do?*—but he could not ask his father" (247). The moment the secret claims Jesse is critical to the formation of his racial identity. The race secret consolidates Jesse's whiteness; he realizes that "everyone, indiscriminately, seemed to be responsible for the fire" (247). Jesse's individuation corresponds with his inscription into the father's law. "Everyone" here invokes the nation, distinguishing the white mob from the lynched body of the black man; Jesse's negotiation of the oedipal requires not a repudiation of either the mother or the father but rather a repudiation of his desire for the black male body. The repression of that homoerotic desire (neither homosexual nor heterosexual, falling outside Freud's narrative of discrete oedipal resolution) binds the white community of the nation.

As he identifies with his father, Jesse's complex is positively resolved and his mother—with whom his wife Grace has already been identified figuratively—is eroticized anew in his imagination. Jesse studies her as she looks on intently at the tortured and naked black man, the "sweet and rotten" (247) odor of his burning flesh spreading across the clearing. "He watched his mother's face. Her eyes were very bright, her mouth was open: she was more beautiful than he had ever seen her, and more strange. He began to feel a joy he had never felt before. He watched the hanging, gleaming body, the most beautiful and terrible object he had ever seen till then" (247). As with the father earlier, Jesse's mother also takes in the scene of the lynching with both eyes and mouth. Identified with his father, to whose body after all he remains coupled, Jesse's "strange" new feelings toward his mother, the "joy he had never felt before," are mediated by the black man's body. She is strangely beautiful (and eroticized) because Jesse has spied her desirous gaze upon the naked body of the black man. He uses the same adjective to describe both his mother and the black man's body: both are "beautiful" to him. As an adult, Jesse's guilt (he too is "responsible for the fire") and forbidden desire are disowned and projected onto the black man in the form of a rape fantasy; the black man becomes the aggressor, ruled by insatiable and boundless sexual appetites.[11]

We witness the scene of castration from the perspective of a child carried on his father's shoulders. Baldwin's account of the mob violence is disarming for its directness, flooding the reader's imagination with awful detail, delivered without respite, yet the description ultimately seems sparse, too. The effect is that of witnessing the violence in real time, rendering the reader short of breath. Returning to study the passage critically, more carefully, the reader is swept into the real time of the violence all over again; the pace of the rushing mob dictates the reader's movement through the description. Jesse's individuation is captured too in the description, delineated in his own feeble resistance, more centrifuge than will, to the irresistible force of the mob. His body is enlisted by whiteness. The process of Jesse's individuation coincides with the consolidation of white indivisibility. He becomes self-aware but only by way of the communion with the white body of his father (literally) and a bloodthirsty mob. Jesse also wishes his hand were the hand belonging to his father's friend, the hand that holds and caresses the cherished fetish object.

Baldwin attributes the castration of the black man to a conflicted white desire to both violently and intimately possess black manhood. Jesse is immediately fascinated by the black penis as impossible fetish object: "One of his father's friends reached up and in his hands he held a knife: and Jesse wished that he had been that man" (247). He wants to violently dispossess the black man of his penis as much as he wants to hold and caress it—and perhaps also as a means to doing just that. His father's hands betray the same erotic desire as Jesse feels them "on his ankles slip and tighten." The black man's privates, severed from his body, accrue only greater fantastic and sensual allure:

> The man with the knife took the nigger's privates in his hand, one hand, still smiling, as though he were weighing them. In the cradle of the one white hand, the nigger's privates seemed as remote as meat being weighed in the scales; but seemed heavier, too, much heavier, and Jesse felt his scrotum tighten; and huge, huge, much bigger than his father's, flaccid, hairless, the largest thing he had ever seen till then, and the blackest. The white hand stretched them, cradled them, caressed them. (247–48)

The use of the euphemism "privates" emphasizes again the child's perspective while also ironizing the impossibility of black self-ownership. Jesse's imagination is stirred not by the lynching but by the black penis as fetish object. The transformation of the black penis into a magic object requires that the racial-sexual violence become naturalized; in other words, the castrate penis must itself become fantastic in order to sanction genocidal violence. Jesse's fascination with the castrate "nigger's privates" betrays his identification of the black man as a competing figure of paternal authority captured by his oedipal imagination. The black man's castration is reproduced syntactically upon the father, whose own "privates" are disincorporated in the mimetically broken grammar of Baldwin's sentence fragment: "and huge, huge, much bigger than his father's [privates], flaccid, hairless, the largest thing he had ever seen till then, and the blackest." The father's "privates"—now truly private—are rendered unnamable, accorded the privacy unavailable to black intimacy yet conditional on the violent and ritualistic publicity of black sexuality. By Baldwin's revisioned oedipal logic, the privileged privacy of white intimacy is conditioned also on the shameful secret of homoerotic racialism, the disavowal of which perpetuates ritualized racist torture and violence. Baldwin's grammar for sexual modernity substitutes the black phallus for that of the white father, imbuing the black male organ with the magic of fetish in compensation for the libidinal desire (mother's, father's, child's) redirected away from the Father. The consolidation of white privacy (shame, humility, civilization) remains contingent upon colonial and white supremacist violence, while coveting the lost (primitive, shameless, perverse) sexuality projected onto the savage(d) body.

The unremitting cultural fixation on the black penis also needs to be understood as a legacy of lynching. The culture of lynching continues to generate fresh enactments of its ritual violence: the separation of the man from the penis, the substitution of penis for the man, the impossibility of a "private" black sexuality, contempt for black humanity. The mythology of the black penis is so deep-rooted in the popular imagination that I find it necessary every time I teach the story to remind my students that "the nigger's privates" are not indeed "the largest thing [Jesse] had ever seen till then." Nor are they "the blackest." And I doubt that I am entirely successful in convincing them.

Jesse's identification with his father positively resolves his oedipal crisis. "His father's face was full of sweat, his eyes were very peaceful. At that moment Jesse loved his father more than he had ever loved him. He felt that his father had carried him through a mighty test, had revealed to him a great secret which would be the key to his life forever" (248). The secret desire for the black man unites Jesse to his father. White supremacy is contingent on blackness and particularly on a fetishized black sexuality. For Baldwin, this is the secret that consolidates whiteness or, more specifically, a white masculinity that transcends the individuation of homosexual and heterosexual identities yet defines sexual modernity. The secret governs the adult Jesse but remains illegible to him:

> Each man, in the thrilling silence which sped outward from their exchanges, their laughter, and their anecdotes, seemed wrestling, in various degrees of darkness, with a secret which he could not articulate to himself, and which, however directly it related to the war, related yet more surely to his privacy and his past. They could no longer be sure, after all, that they had all done the same things. They had never dreamed that their privacy could contain any element of terror, could threaten, that is, to reveal itself, to the scrutiny of a judgment day, while remaining unreadable and inaccessible to themselves; nor had they dreamed that the past, while certainly refusing to be forgotten, could yet so stubbornly refuse to be remembered. (238)

The threat of greater black mobility threatens the white supremacy enjoyed by Jesse and his friends, and this threat unifies them in their "war." However, it is the elaborate sexual desire for the black man that profoundly consolidates the union between white men. Baldwin never specifies the referent for the pronoun "they." The racialized desire that consolidates white masculinity confounds that identity so that it cannot (dares not) name itself. Shame is formative too in regard to the white heterosexual male. What I find useful about this story is its location of a nexus between racialization and sexuality in the formation of whiteness. Baldwin demonstrates how white supremacist fantasies about the black male body construct forms of white masculinity that are not necessarily heterosexual. We learn in the story that Jesse's desire for the black man is integral to his oedipal phase. He will desire the black man both as love object and as the object of an aggressive, cannibalistic identification, regardless of how the complex finds resolution. Desire for the black man's body generates white male sexualities. According to Baldwin's oedipal formula, rescripted for the American scene, the (white) male child's identifications and desires vis-à-vis his mother and father are mediated by a black male body. In its resolution, the complex generates multiple (male) sexualities, but all of these sexualities, regardless of their divergent trajectories, necessarily contract a singular, indivisible whiteness.

Baldwin's story suggests that homoerotic interracialism functions as a common denominator for modern male heterosexual and homosexual identities. There are gaps and problems here, not least of which are those inherited from the classic oedipal formulation. The story emphatically focuses on white male racial/sexual identity. Since I share that focus in this essay, it should be clear that I do find it critically important and useful. The risk lies in the tendency to elide female sexualities and lives in the process of theorizing male sexual identities. The reiteration of the oedipal in Baldwin's story renders female sexuality generic and secondary. Baldwin situates the mythologized black male body as the singular site from which white masculinities violently erupt. This emphasis in particular on lynching and castration reinforces historical silences surrounding the institutionalized rape of black women. Baldwin's race-conscious reformulation of the oedipal complex limits considerations of how historically state-sanctioned sexual violence against black women might also locate a nexus for the formation of U.S. race, gender, and sexual identities. The specificity of Baldwin's subject in "Going to Meet the Man" is crucial and instructive. But that specificity does not necessarily foreclose the tendency to universalize; here the universalizing arises from the investments of black masculinity in situating the spectacle of lynching as the most powerful symbol for the history of racial violence in the United States. As Hazel Carby observes, "the institutionalized rape of black women has never been as powerful a symbol of black oppression as the spectacle of lynching."[12]

This returns me to the problem of rippling silences to which I referred at the beginning of this chapter. Why the absence of images of Iraqi women prisoners? Just a quick history of the circulation of the Abu Ghraib images: the photographs were first made public on April 28, 2004, on American network television, in a report aired by the CBS news magazine program *60 Minutes II*. Soon after, some of the images were published in the magazine the *New Yorker*, on May 10, 2004, in an article by Seymour Hersh. The photos immediately exploded on the Internet, creating an international scandal for the Bush administration. In fact, even before the April 28 release of the photos, the American Civil Liberties Union sought release of prisoner abuse photos and other documents, filing a Freedom of Information Act request with the federal government on October 7, 2003. The selective release of images from Abu Ghraib prompted a lawsuit by the ACLU. Regardless of repeated legal victories by the ACLU, the federal government has continued to withhold images and documents. After new images were somehow leaked, airing on Australian television in February of 2006, the United States declared that it would stop fighting the full disclosure of the images. However, the ACLU reports that the Pentagon still holds twenty-nine additional images documenting torture at locations in Afghanistan and Iraq. The ACLU is demanding that the Obama administration honor the 2008 decision from a federal appeals court ordering that the Bush administration release all images. At the time, the Bush administration argued that making additional photos public would "generate outrage and would violate US obligations towards detainees under the Geneva Conventions."[13] In other words, the government's argument is that it refuses to release images in order to protect the dignity, the humanity, of the subjects of those images. Remarkable also is the Bush administration's appeal to the Geneva Conventions, which it otherwise flagrantly, famously disregarded. This alibi, however, is astutely borrowed by the U.S. government from its own critics. Even with the independent release of new images on Australian television and elsewhere, pictures of women prisoners are consistently included among those deemed too graphic or too sensitive.

While this tension between the need for witness and the violence of looking is more pervasive when it comes to the images of women prisoners at Abu Ghraib, it is not limited to those images. British writer and political commentator Richard Webster reports on the complaints by readers to editors of the newspaper the *Guardian* regarding the publication on its cover of a photograph of a naked male prisoner cowering in front of attacking military dogs. Webster quotes the defense of the cover provided by Ian Mayes, an editor for the paper: "Taken with other photographs, and we know there are at least 1,800, many showing greater abuses, the picture has an imperative that demands prominent publication—and demands it, apparently, regardless of all consequences (for instance the further excitement of anti-American feeling in the Arab world)."

Webster takes Mayes to task for what he reads as an instrumental slippage from incitement to excitement: "The choice of the word 'excitement' when normal usage would be 'incitement' is itself odd. One suspects that one of the reasons Mayes has shied away from the natural choice of the words is that 'incitement' is commonly used with 'hatred.'" Webster's dispute with Mayes's argument is the sloughing off of any accountability for what repercussions might follow the publication of an incendiary image that he reads in Mayes's rhetorical exchange of "excitement" for "incitement." In ending, I want to hold on, however, to Mayes's use of the word "excitement" a bit longer, harking back to the repeated use of the word by Baldwin to signal in his story of white racial formation a persistent sexual undercurrent. It is excitement and not incitement that is on display in lynching photographs and the photos from Abu Ghraib. But is it also excitement that discomfits readers of the *Guardian*? What is it about the shamelessness of the torturers in the photos that seems simultaneously to shame and fascinate spectators of the photos? Reports about the abuses at Abu Ghraib were already widespread before the release of the images, but outrage in the United States was only incited by the circulation of images of those abuses. As with Baldwin's narrative (and even the critical response or lack thereof to his story), the race secret is infectious, rippling out onto the nation, and onto a Western coalition organized by the U.S. war machine, as it excitedly consumed the images of abuse, at once homophobic and homoerotic, but seemed just as quickly to retreat into some kind of closet. I end with questions that still haunt me: why are images of torture of Iraqi women withheld from spectacle relative to the globally publicized companion images of men? Do they incite or excite? If they excite, do they excite differently than the images of tortured male bodies with which we became so familiar in the spring of 2004? Do they shame the spectator any differently? How are national and colonial constructions of race, gender, and sexuality consolidated or disturbed in the circulation or withholding of these images?

Many commentators, both on the Left and on the Right, apologists and critics of U.S. imperialism alike, described the Abu Ghraib photos as pornographic. Left critiques of the images as pornographic typically implicated straight pornography, since the definitions of pornography bandied about in these critiques reflect a longstanding heteronormative bias characteristic of the more polemically sexphobic strains of antipornography rhetoric. In her article on the sexual politics of Abu Ghraib, Mary Ann Tétreault, for instance, defines pornography as "a record of the violation of a subject's physical and psychic integrity."[14] She adds that "many Abu Ghraib images also are pornographic in the conventional sense. Their subjects are naked and lewdly posed" (34). Setting aside these polemical and generalized definitions of pornography, I wonder still if the classification of the images as pornographic obscures (protects from greater scrutiny, that is) the erotics of the images. The reduction of the violence of Abu Ghraib to a generalized notion of the pornographic occludes the racialized erotics of U.S. empire. Audre Lorde, in her essay on "The Uses of the Erotic," famously opposes the pornographic to the erotic, situating the former as a patriarchal and misogynist corruption of the latter. But to say that the pornographic is a corruption of the erotic is also to trace in the pornographic the residual of the erotic. What shift do we make in our hermeneutic if we read the Abu Ghraib photos not as pornography but as an imperial homoerotics?

The antipornography rhetoric frames the conversation within a moral universe that is itself potentially already complicit with modes of U.S. empire. By shifting the terms of analysis from the pornographic to the erotic, I also propose reading the Abu Ghraib images not as aberrations but as constructions symptomatic of the homoerotics of empire. Hence, to implicate the images within an abiding, historical practice of instrumentalized, U.S. imperial homoerotics is also to understand their constitutive function in relation to nation and empire.

The antipornography feminist stance that equates all porn with gendered violence has the effect also of isolating the Abu Ghraib images from their erotic and homosocial economies. In effect, such an antipornography argument may actually obstruct a more comprehensive analysis of the violence at Abu Ghraib as a permanent condition of U.S. empire rather than a consequence of the derivative pornographic imaginations of isolated actors. As I mentioned in framing this chapter, one of the challenges of reading those images of abuse that first reached mass audiences in May of 2004 is cautiously negotiating analogy in order to situate Abu Ghraib properly within a legacy of state-sanctioned racist violence.

From a critical legal perspective, the prison abuses at Abu Ghraib, officially excused as the misdeeds of a few "bad apples," might also be understood as what Scott Michaelsen refers to as a "permanent state of racial emergency" (89). Like Colin Dayan, Michaelsen looks to constitutional law in order to trace the history of its inconsistent application of equal protection and due process. For Michaelsen, the USA PATRIOT Act, the order for Japanese internment during World War II, and the history of aggressive search and seizure along the U.S.-Mexico borderlands all exemplify "the permanent state of racial exception." A liberal critique of legislation such as the USA PATRIOT Act neglects the larger history of de facto racist exceptionalism that is constitutive of American freedom and democracy.

The images from Abu Ghraib require a hermeneutic similar to Michaelsen's—one that understands their seeming exceptionalism as symptomatic. The nature of the condemnation, a nation-wide handwringing over practices of sexual humiliation (and more precisely, the perceived homosexual character of those practices), indicate for Puar a collective, national evasion of the full horror of physical torture, not to mention war. The "spectacular question," Puar determines, is that the "sexual excess such as sodomy and oral sex as well as S/M practices" are what register public moral outrage, as opposed to ravages of war that also include "the slow starvation of millions due to the UN sanctions against Iraq, the deaths of thousands of Iraqi civilians since the U.S. invasions in April 2003, or the plundering and carnage in Falluja" (*Terrorist Assemblages*, 79). Puar links the exceptionalism of this moral outrage to what she terms "the sanctity of the sexual" within liberalism: "the sexual is the ultimate site of violation, portrayed as extreme in relation to the individual rights of privacy and ownership accorded to the body within liberalism" (81). But might we then not ask how ritualized sexual violence is deployed as a means of securing self-ownership and privacy for some bodies, while depriving others of the same? In other words, we should be asking how these images speak to the erotics of U.S. empire.

Puar takes to task the critiques by white gay men who continue to claim shame as a unique and privileged affective territory. Patrick Moore, in particular, reads the Abu Ghraib images as a further assault by the state on the dignity of gay men—meaning of course white gay men. Puar chides Moore for his assumption that the Arab men in the photographs must be straight. He also assumes that U.S. gay spectators are, if not white, at the very least non-Arab and/or non-Muslim. Furthermore, as Puar also indicates, it remains unimaginable to Moore that any of the torturers could be gay or lesbian Americans:

> Is it really prudent to unequivocally foreclose the chance that there might be a gay man or lesbian among the perpetrators of the torture at Abu Ghraib? To foreground homophobia over other vectors of shame—this foregrounding functioning as a key symptom of homonormativity—is to miss that these photos are not merely representative of the homophobia of the military: they are also racist, misogynist, and imperialist.

The problem Puar identifies is similar to the one I locate in the first page of Sedgwick's *Epistemology* and one endemic to much—but not all—gay and lesbian politics: a collapsing of antihomophobia with an uncritical homophilia. I would amend Puar's piercing analysis only to add the possibility of a link between the question she poses about the likelihood of a gay prison guard at Abu Ghraib and her observation that the photos are not just homophobic but also "racist, misogynist, and imperialist." My assertion throughout this book is that U.S. nationalism did not so much marginalize as instrumentalize modern gay male identity. The late-twentieth-century homonationalism of Puar's analysis then represents only the latest, neoliberal turn of a longstanding phenomenon.

For Puar, the fixing of a Western public's attention on what it perceives as simulated gay sex speaks to the marked inability (and resistance) of that public to appreciate the full effects of the torture on the bodies, minds, and spirits of the Iraqi men pictured in the images. According to Puar, Western responses to the photos have unduly privileged sexuality over gender: "The simulated sex acts must be thought of in terms of gendered roles rather than through a universalizing notion of sexual orientation" (97). I agree with Puar that popular and critical responses have mostly neglected the gendered constructions of power enacted in the scenes of torture; however, shifting the question entirely from sexuality to gender serves only to universalize a different constellation. Puar turns to victim's advocacy discourse in order to argue that, as with rape, the torture at Abu Ghraib needs to be understood not as sex but violence. Yet it strikes me that Puar herself is not entirely convinced by this position and that her analysis of the "faggot Muslim body" complicates it considerably. She raises a more compelling—for my purposes at least—related point in her insistence that we put pressure on reading the torture as a simulation of gay sex exclusively. "Saying that the simulated and actual sex scenes replicate gay sex is an easy way for all—mass media, Orientalist anthropologists, the military establishment, LGBTIQ groups and organizations—to disavow the supposedly perverse proclivities inherent in heterosexual sex and the gender normativity immanent in some kinds of gay sex" (97).

Building on Puar's argument, we might also say that the images from Abu Ghraib—as well as Baldwin's portrait of lynching culture—reveal how a "national-normative sexuality" originates from a violently racialized erotics. That racial erotics haunts the supposedly rigid boundaries of sexual orientation and gender normativity.

I borrow the notion of "national-normative sexuality" and its counterpart, "antinational sexuality," from Brian Keith Axel's study of torture in Punjab, which Puar also finds critically valuable:

> I propose that torture in Punjab is a practice of repeated and violent circumscription that produces not only sexed bodies, but also a form of sexual differentiation. This is not a differentiation between categories of male and female, but between what may be called national-normative sexuality and antinational sexuality. . . . National-normative sexuality provides the sanctioned heterosexual means for reproducing the nation's community. Torture casts national-normative sexuality as a fundamental modality of citizen production in relation to an antinational sexuality that postulates sex as "cause" of not only sexual experience but also of subversive behavior and extraterritorial desire. (quoted in Puar 98–99)

The history of U.S. racial subjugation, as evidenced by Baldwin's depiction of lynching culture and the sanctioned rape of black women as well as by the genocidal practices necessitated by its self-authorizing occupation of indigenous lands, constitute a form of state-sanctioned torture or, as Axel puts it, a "repeated and violent circumscription" that yields the sexed, raced, and gendered bodies of the nation and its others. Puar uses Axel's argument to elaborate on what she terms the "monster-terrorist-fag": "the (homo)sexual perversions of the terrorist is also a priori constituted as stateless, lacking national legitimization and national boundaries" (99). A similar logic characterizes the history of European colonization of indigenous lands and the genocidal policies of the U.S. state toward the indigenous nations it seeks perpetually to delegitimize. Puar adapts Axel's theory to the circumstances at Abu Ghraib, focusing on national differentiation not strictly as sexual differentiation but rather as gender differentiation, a means of feminizing and ultimately racing the terrorist body: "Torture, to compound Axel's formulation, works not only to disaggregate national from antinational sexualities . . . but also, in accordance with nationalist fantasies, to reorder gender and, in the process, to corroborate implicit racial hierarchies" (100).

At Abu Ghraib, the aggressive heteronormative masculinity of male soldiers exposes a constitutive homoerotic underside to imperial sexuality. Puar asks, "why talk about sex at all? Was anyone having sex in these photos?" (97). We might read her questions as rhetorical—a critique of the West's misplaced focus on the simulated gay sex choreographed by prison guards over the physical pain of prisoners and the subsequent erasure of the torture and rape of Iraqi women and children. It is crucial that we investigate, as Puar does, the common ideological underpinnings at work when pundits across a seemingly broad political spectrum isolate Abu Ghraib's scenes of simulated gay sex—as evidence either of the military's homophobia or of the depravity of U.S. or Western culture—from the mass violence, including rape, precipitated by war and U.S. imperialism. However, the question Puar poses—"Was anyone having sex in these photos?"—is not moot. In order to trace the repurposing of pleasure and desire for conquest and for the consolidation of a national-normative sexuality as the definitive marker of civilization, I take her question at face value.

Perhaps no one is having sex in those photos, but that question needs to remain open. At the very least, torture at Abu Ghraib mobilized an erotic, one that excited the torturers and much of their spectatorship. As Seymour Hersh reports in the *New Yorker*, the images were "swapped from computer to computer throughout the 320th Battalion."[15] The staging of the scene for digital photography, the act of picture taking, and the sharing of the images—the act of hitting "send"—all comprise elements of the torturers' erotic, one that finds an obvious predecessor in lynching photography.

Perhaps even more so than the outright ban on homosexuality, the tellingly hysterical policy of "Don't Ask, Don't Tell" (DADT) suggests the military's anxiety that manifesting its own structural homosexualism— naming it, publicizing it within and outside its ranks, de-secreting it— might dislodge the disarticulated desire of homoerotic racialism from its constitutive center in the soldier's and imperial nation's unconscious, neutralizing its historical serviceability. Of course, as Jasbir Puar establishes in her discussion of homonationalism, there is little threat that bringing the homosexual out of the closet (not to mention inviting him or her into the offices of power) will disrupt the war machine. The mobilization of national gay and lesbian organizations around the repeal of DADT and marriage equality recalls once again the necessity for insisting on the critical distinction between a call for homophilia and a movement against homophobia, especially in its genocidal deployments against populations designated by "anti-national sexuality."

3

The Global Taste for Queer

For me, teaching queer film and media today involves a will-
ingness to be challenged by texts such as Deepa Mehta's 1996
film *Fire* and Tomás Gutiérrez Alea and Juan Carlos Tabío's
1994 film *Strawberry and Chocolate*, both of which lend
themselves to analysis from within the discourses and theories elaborated to engage U.S. films while suggesting that
they are indifferent to those theories.
—Kara Keeling, in Bronski et al., "Queer Film and Media
Pedagogy"

In his contribution to Arnaldo Cruz-Malavé's and Martin Manalansan's
collection *Queer Globalizations: Citizenship and the Afterlife of Colonialism* (2002), Joseba Gabilondo charts the emergence in the 1990s of a
"global taste" for queer film. Following the unexpected success of films
such as *Farewell, My Concubine* (1993) and *Priscilla, Queen of the Desert*
(1994), film industries internationally (both corporate and state spon-
sored) capitalized on a newly commodified, traveling form of queerness
in the form of narrative cinema. Typically, a nationalist or local context
authenticates the narrative, which, nonetheless, relies on a deterritorialized reception both for its commercial success and its representative
global queerness. Among his examples, Gabilondo cites Tomás Gutiérrez Alea and Juan Carlos Tabío's *Fresa y chocolate*, which debuted in
Cuba late in 1993 before making the rounds of numerous international
film festivals in 1994 to wide critical and popular acclaim, eventually
being nominated for an Academy Award for Best Foreign Film. The
film's globality depends on how readily it assimilates a universalizable
queerness. Gutiérrez Alea and Tabio's direction invites a touristic con-

sumption of Cuba (more specifically, Havana) in order to hail a queer spectatorship, negotiating in the formation of that spectator-subject a dialectic between the brown exotic and the gay cosmopolitan.

An analysis of Anglo American spectatorship of the film tracks the meeting of the gay cosmopolitan and his exotic other, tracing the violence of that encounter. My concern in this chapter is with the local particularities (i.e., Cuban or Habanero *mariconeria, homosexualidad*, etc.) potentially lost (mistranslated) in the move to the transnational, in this instance a queer globality. A parallel dynamic occurs, I argue, with the recuperation of Jose Martí's 1891 essay "Nuestra America," by American Studies scholars eager, ironically, to explode the nationalist bias at the origins of the discipline.[1]

Martí's essay provides New Americanists with an anti-imperialist remapping of the hemisphere that situates the United States as the "other America," that interloping *"pueblo rubio del continente"* that seeks to displace the *"hombres biliosos y trigueños"* of *nuestra America*.[2] It is impossible to appreciate the constructions of heterosexual and queer masculinities in *Fresa y chocolate* without reference to the nation-founding mythologies that Martí's essay initiates. Martí's essay originates an Ariel/Caliban trope that informs constructions of Cuban masculinity. The figures of the gay cosmopolitan and parochial communist youth can also be read as extensions of the Ariel/Caliban trope. Failure to recognize the legacy of that trope recenters an Anglo American perspective, sanctioning an uncomplicated identification between the gay cosmopolitan spectator and Diego, the exotic Cuban-cum-gay-cosmopolitan hero. As Kara Keeling points out,

> a heightened critical awareness of "queer" as a marker of difference in disparate locations, coupled with the global availability of "queer films" produced in sociocultural contexts different from those of the United States, necessitates, it seems to me, the development of queer media pedagogies capable of attending to the particularities of articulations of "queer" sexualities from different locations without imposing on them specifically

U.S. notions of "lesbian and gay" sociopolitical and cultural formations. (Bronski et al. 124)

Unlike their Western counterparts, for instance, many gay Cuban spectators did not identify with Diego, and the film may in fact hold quite different cultural and political significance for them.

Reviewers of *Fresa y chocolate* frequently compared it to *Kiss of the Spider Woman* (1985) and *The Wedding Banquet* (1993). David Stratton of *Variety*, for instance, comments on the film's potential global appeal: "Filled with malicious swipes against the Castro regime, it's a provocative but very humane comedy about sexual opposites and, with proper handling, could attract the *Wedding Banquet* crowd in cinemas worldwide."[3] Stratton was accurate in forecasting the Cuban film's international success. In addition to its Academy Award nomination, it also won Best Picture at the Berlin and Gramado film festivals.[4] *Fresa y chocolate* and predecessors such as *The Wedding Banquet* and *Kiss of the Spider Woman* now belong to an archive of gay cosmopolitanism; however, as Gabilondo points out, "these queer films respond to very different foreign national agendas and sociopolitical situations" (236). Distributed in the United States by Miramax, the film lists Mexican and Spanish coproducers; hence, to some degree, its production as well as its consumption was an international "affair." What seems to get lost, however, in this articulation of a gay cosmopolitanism is the specifically Cuban locality of the film. Stratton's claim that the film is "filled with malicious swipes against the Castro regime" echoes the popular reception of the film as an expression of internal resistance and protest; the problem with this reading is that it elides the material and political reality of the film's production by the Cuban Institute of the Arts and Films Industry (ICAIC) during the *periodo especial* (or "special period"), a time of severe economic crisis in Cuba following the collapse of the Soviet Union. Stratton's review in fact is especially egregious although not entirely atypical in its ahistoricity.[5] My concern then is with how the "global taste for queer" vanishes the local queer realities it would purportedly represent but also with how those local sexualities already form part of a more historically dynamic erotic circuitry. It is more useful to think not so much in terms of a parochialized local but rather in terms of something more akin to what Bruce Robbins calls a "messy compromised particularity."[6] I don't mean to absolutely dismiss gay cosmopolitanism but wish rather to redirect it critically, as Gabilondo does when he examines how the emergence of a global queer cinema in the 1990s functions to negotiate "different national situations and globalization . . . us[ing] the same discursive strategy of mobilizing a desiring male queer character in order to relegitimize and articulate a new global hegemony around the different national masculinities and hegemonies set in crisis by globalization" (236–37).

It is also critical to complicate any simple touristic reading of the film as an authentic representation of queer Cuban identities, since the film also belongs to the catalogue of queer globality itemized by Gabilondo. Several critics take a more cynical stance. Regarding the film's international success, Ricardo Ortiz argues that "the release of *Strawberry and Chocolate* in the West functions somewhat as a commercial gesture of good will to its new trading partners; official homophobic policy on the island serves as an issue which might see progress more readily than other complicated political problems Cuba faces."[7] I agree partially with Ortiz's assessment that the film is "meant to appeal directly, perhaps exclusively, to a metropolitan sensibility in the developed world" ("Docile Bodies," 92). The great success of the film in Cuba disproves the idea that the filmmakers directed their work "exclusively" to the West. The film, I argue, is coded for both international and local audiences. Nonetheless, it is important to consider how exactly the film reaches its Western audiences, especially a "gay international" that embraced and celebrated it. As Charles Nero points out, "*Fresa y chocolate* became one of the first Cuban films specifically marketed to an international audience. This type of marketing affects the themes, narratives, and other cinematic devices employed in order to gain a broad, international audience."[8]

I first saw *Fresa y chocolate* in September of 1994, as part of the 32nd New York Film Festival. The audience was composed almost entirely of gay white men who, at the film's conclusion, stood in ovation for Gutiérrez Alea, in attendance with the actress Mirta Ibarra, his wife. In the film Ibarra portrays Nancy, the prostitute who becomes romantically and sexually linked with David, the impressionable communist youth played by Vladimir Cruz. Jorge Perugorria portrays the ostracized homosexual Diego, whom the narrative seemingly is required to expel from Cuba at the film's conclusion. The relationship between David and Nancy provides the narrative with a safe, heterosexual resolution, saving each character from the sexual corruptions of prostitution and homosexuality. I was stunned at the conclusion of the film, which I found transparently conservative in its sexual politics, to hear men seated around me weeping. Perhaps most startling (but maybe predictable too) was the fact that I had observed many of these same men ignore or—once they'd passed through the doors of Alice Tully Hall—glibly ridicule among themselves the small number of gay Cuban exiles politely disseminating flyers outside the screening with information about the gay and lesbian Cuban artists, writers, and filmmakers who had been persecuted and/or expelled by the Cuban government. This modest demonstration could hardly compare with the notoriously aggressive politics of organizations like the Cuban American National Foundation, yet the demonstrators clearly were dismissed as representative right-wing zealots. The gay men in the audience then identified with Diego's sentimental fiction, while dismissing the actual sexual dissidents his character represents. What played out at Alice Tully Hall that Sunday afternoon was the refusal of a white, Anglo American gay audience to imaginatively and responsibly witness a queer alterity outside its own cultural register. Gay spectators in the audience identified with the representation of Diego as a gay cosmopolitan, someone who shared the same cultural archive, the same trademarked sensibilities. Gay Cuban men did not necessarily identify with Diego. As José Quiroga recounts, "gays among the movie audience whistled and cajoled not Diego or David, but David's dour, dogmatic friend" (Quiroga 144). Meanwhile, popular queer reception internationally absolutely relied on identification with Diego. Furthermore, as Carrie Hamilton points out, "By allowing two acclaimed heterosexual directors to make the film, the Cuban Film Institute (ICAIC) was able to present itself as liberal while continuing to prevent homosexual-identified directors from making homosexual-themed films."[9] Ian Lumsden as well observes that while Gutiérrez Alea was able to make a film with a gay character, ICAIC "simultaneously blocked all attempts by its gay members . . . to produce work with gay themes."[10]

Not only does Diego order strawberry ice cream on the day when chocolate is on the menu at Coppelia; he drinks tea instead of coffee. When David refuses tea in favor of coffee, Diego mocks, "Civilized people drink tea, but not us. We [Cubans] prefer coffee." He sings, "Todos los negros tomamos café." The taste for coffee is associated with blackness. Diego's rejection of coffee rehearses for Cuban audiences Cuba's postrevolutionary political and cultural affiliations with African internationalism while confirming his disidentification with blackness. The Cuban national culture to which Diego's nostalgia harkens is represented by the baroque postmodernism of José Lezama Lima's novel *Paradiso*. While Diego (indirectly) provides a critique of the stultifying mode of socialist realism enforced by the state during the "special period" (the film is set in 1979, but speaks to the realities of the early 1990s), the alternative aesthetic he proposes (baroque, nostalgic, European) erodes any foundation for a sustained critique. Consistent with the tradition of melodrama from which it draws, the film presents characters at once two-dimensional yet imbued with great paradox. Diego's dissidence is isolated and rendered impotent. His desire for David is converted into a desexualized paternalism as he arranges for him to lose his virginity with Nancy—in Diego's own bed.

During their first meeting, Diego assails a nonplussed David with a litany of gay cosmopolitan icons: Maria Callas, Oscar Wilde, García Lorca. While Anglo American audiences encounter a projection of their own identities on the screen (albeit a rather stereotypical one), within a Cuban national narrative, Diego registers as an exotic, ill suited to Cuba's tropical and revolutionary climates. If Diego provides gay filmgoers with a cosmopolitan figure, David presents the primitive brown body of cosmopolitan desire. In a local context, David also figures the national body: masculine, infused with the nation's hybrid vigor, sensible but unsophisticated. The Ariel/Caliban logic of Paz's characterization, along with other cultural markers, codes David as hybrid. Charles Nero, for instance, also points out that "David is a *guajiro*, someone from the Cuban countryside where racial mixing is more commonplace than it is in the upper classes. Therefore the purity of his racial ancestry is more dubious than the urbane and aristocratic Diego's" (Nero 62).

Gutiérrez Alea and Tabio's direction too encourages the gay cosmopolitan's identificatory projection into the narrative; the cinematography, with its slow pans of Havana's architecture and people, invites a touristic gaze. In a voice-over, David muses philosophically about sexuality, while the camera follows Cuban women sashaying down the street followed by the leers of Cuban men. *Cubanidad* is resolutely identified as heterosexual and *machista*, mediated through David's eyes. If the narrative depends on a deterritorialized reception to succeed as global queer cinema, the film's mise en scène trades on the exoticization of Cuba to appeal to colonial fantasies about the primitive and the brown. The "taste of Havana" provides the cultural capital upon which an abstracted, deterritorialized global queer constituency is mortgaged.

I avoided writing about *Fresa y chocolate* for so many years mostly to avoid the inevitable (and unproductive) polemics that erupt around discussion of Cuba, and perhaps especially the topic of homosexuality in Cuba. Cuba remains a fetish object, especially in an Anglo American context. Paul Julian Smith argues that the

"idea" of Cuba served as a projection or . . . "identification" for leftists in the US and the UK who suffered in the 1980s under triumphalist governments of the Right. For France and Spain, on the other hand, which spent most of the decade under self-styled Socialist administrations, Cuba had ceased for many to be the fetish it had been in the 1960s.[11]

I concur with Smith's appraisal of the late-twentieth-century sociohistorical conditions that have determined how the gleam on Cuba as fetish object waxes and wanes; however, I would argue that the consideration of Cuba as fetish should seriously undertake not only an investigation of the erotic investments of an Anglo American imagination in Cuba but also the more dynamic counterpoint of Cuban/U.S./hemispheric nationalisms, sexualities, and modernities rendered illegible by this fetish's restrictive hermeneutic. Returning to Martí's essay as a nation-founding text is critical for complicating that hermeneutic.

The theme of seduction in *Fresa y chocolate*, the gay cosmopolitan's seduction of the provincial communist youth, uncannily mirrors both the project of reconciliation to which the Cuban state deployed the film internationally as well as the Anglo American projection of erotic desire onto a fetishized Cuba.[12] Carrie Rickey of the *Philadelphia Inquirer*, for instance, reads in *Fresa y chocolate* "a cry from the hearts of Cubans aimed for the hearts of Americans. And it's a bull's-eye."[13] Uncannily, this culturally chauvinistic response may well hit the mark itself. While it may not occur to Rickey that the film has a Cuban audience and potentially conflicting receptions in Cuba and abroad, she happens on a dialectic that shapes Cuban nationalism and does indeed unravel as a kind of romantic tension. The dynamic between Diego, the Europeanized, feminine aesthete, and David, the masculine and organic representative of the nation, invokes the opposition between the Caliban and Ariel of Shakespeare's *Tempest*, as it is reiterated in Roberto Fernández Retamar's essay "Caliban" and arguably prefigured by José Martí in his most famous essay, "Nuestra America."[14] Caliban represents for Retamar the masculinist ideal of "Che" Guevara's "New Man"; not incidentally, the title of the short story from which the film is adapted is "El lobo, el bosque, y el hombre Nuevo" or "The Wolf, the Forest, and the New Man." Both the story and its screenplay adaptation were written by Senel Paz. As Ricardo Ortiz argues in an essay on the legacies of Retamar's Calibanic school, "The jump, then, from 'New Man' rhetoric to the instrumental but no less tropic invocation of Caliban by Retamar is a short one."[15] On the opposition between Caliban (or the New Man) and Ariel, Ortiz draws attention to the "feminization or hysterization" of those male intellectuals Retamar rejects: "The Ariel figure itself, rejected ostensibly for its traditional association with a willing servitude to the master, is often also figured as the 'airy,' obsequious feminine counterpart to the roughly recalcitrant (and potentially rapacious) Caliban" ("Revolution's Other Histories," 37).

Paz revised the screenplay ten times before it was finally accepted by the ICAIC. David, resolutely heterosexual in Gutiérrez Alea's adaptation, is more ambiguously drawn in Paz's story. Both film and story provide David's perspective; however, the naturalistic style of Gutiérrez Alea's film cannot convey the unreliable narrator of Paz's story nor its ambiguities. David's self-questioning is not represented in the film, while in the story he probes into his motivations for visiting Diego: "Spell it out slowly and clearly, David Alvarez, why, if you were a real man, had you gone to the home of a homosexual; if you were a revolutionary, to the home of a counter-revolutionary, and if you were an atheist, why had you gone to the home of a believer?"[16] The film adaptation not only introduces a heterosexual romance to resolve ambiguities around David's sexuality but also—perhaps too anxiously—opens the narrative with an explicit scene of intercourse between a man and woman spied by David in the same hotel where he hopes to seduce his fiancée, Vivian. Its too-anxious heterosexuality is precisely the queerest quality of the film. Scholarship on the film, and more generally on homosexuality in Castro's Cuba, tends to focus on the particulars of Cuba's revolutionary dogma and/or generalizations about Latin American homosexuality (which ultimately tell us more about the fantasies of gay cosmopolitanism than about sexual practices in Latin America). As an alternative, I follow Emilio Bejel's example in tracing the "problematic image of the queer . . . [to] Cuba's struggle for independence from both Spanish colonialism and US neocolonialism."[17] As Bejel asserts, "the notion of homosexuality and homoeroticism is inscribed, by negation, in the prescriptive models of the national Cuban narrative. . . . [D]espite—or perhaps because of—the enormous efforts to expel the queer body, the specter of homosexuality has always haunted Cuban national discourse" (xiv–xv). I add to Bejel's formulation the specter of miscegenation, which, as Siobhan Sommerville has argued, intersects with and compounds Victorian discourse on sexual inversion.[18] The invert and mulatto or mestizo are the kissing cousins of hemispheric genealogies of the nation in the Americas. As Carrie Hamilton points out, "critics of *Strawberry and Chocolate*, while quick to point out the film's stereotypical portrayal of gender and sexuality, usually fail to engage with its racial politics" (259). It is useful to read the film next to Martí's "Our America" in order to engage both the particularities of its racial politics and its articulations of queer sexualities.

Perhaps no Cuban text enacts this confounding of homosexuality and miscegenation as emphatically (or anxiously) as José Martí's "Our America." Martí's essay functions as a polemic, negotiating (and erasing) the race problem in Cuba in order to consolidate a Cuban nationalism and rouse the movement for independence from Spain. Martí proclaims in the final paragraph of the essay that "[t]here can be no racial hate, because there are no races." ("No hay odios de razas, porque no hay razas.")[19] In order to arrive at this utopian ideal, Martí tropes on the mestizo, collapsing the entire history of miscegenation in the Americas into a singular (and metaphorical) figure. Although Martí argues that the emergence of "*nuestra América mestiza*" hails the end of racial difference and consequently the end of "racial hate," his utopic (paradoxically deracialized) vision requires the cooption of the very real, racialized body of the mestizo. Although his polemical essay quite clearly means to inspire a popular nationalist sentiment that will provoke Cubans to rise against Spain and resist the impending U.S. imperialism, "Our America" is equally motivated by the race problem. I want to underscore here the tension between the metaphorically "mottled" body ("*cuerpo pinto*") that Martí fathers in the essay and the material bodies of the mestizo *and* the mulatto. It is the racial demographics of Cuba that make Martí's choice of the category "mestizo" as the embodiment for this nascent American identity both conspicuous and suspect. The word "mestizo" designates a person of mixed European and American Indian ancestry. Clearly, if he is addressing miscegenation in Cuba, the word "mulatto" would much more accurately describe the history of race mixture in Cuba and the racial demographics of the island. The pronounced absence of the mulatto in the essay broadcasts his very significant presence in the geopolitical and psychic space of Martí's *nuestra America*.

"Our America" is often read as prophetic and cited as a testament to Martí's remarkable political insight. However, the essay reveals not only a legitimate concern about future relations between the United States and an independent Cuba but also the anxiety among elite white Creoles concerning Cuba's place among modern nations: "Con los pies en el rosario, la cabeza blanca y el cuerpo pinto de indio y criollo, vinimos, denodados, al mundo de las naciones." ("With the rosary as our guide, our head white and our body mottled, both Indian and Creole, we intrepidly entered the community of nations.") The pronoun "we" refers to the recently independent nations of Latin America, but again the objective here is to inspire a revolutionary sentiment specifically in Cuba. The symbolic mestizo, whose head after all is white, vanquishes the flesh-and-blood mulatto, whose presence would not only publicize the actual racial composition of the island but also situate Cuba within the dominant narratives of degeneration associated at the time with miscegenation and tropicalization. Martí compensates for Cuba's inability to measure up to the standards for progress set forth by the United States and Europe by reducing the contrast between Cuba and its present and future colonizers to a contest of masculinity. He sets out to both exoticize and feminize the European or white man.

Of course, Martí himself is white. The essay accomplishes a disavowal of whiteness for the white Creole. The publication of the essay is only four years removed from emancipation. White Creoles opportunistically disown their whiteness, at least rhetorically, at this moment of nation founding, while continuing to reap the dividends of an entrenched racial hierarchy. The white Creole has disavowed whiteness by adopting the accoutrements of the Indian. If only the white fraction of the components for a mestizo population exists, clearly Martí's mestizo America will never materialize in Cuba. What I wish to emphasize is that the Cuban reader realizes that the embrace of the mestizo as a cultural identity in this essay de facto catapults the white Creole to a position of cultural dominance. The exoticizing of the Spanish, French, or North American in the essay, accomplished by emphasizing differences in speech, attire, and gender performance, confounded with racial/ethnic type, functions to transform the white Creole into a dusky native, distancing him from his colonial past. At the same time, that birthright is not extended to Cuba's black and mulatto population who cannot contribute any fraction to the mestizo body.

The Madrilenian and Parisian are represented as dandies: "They cannot reach the first limb with their puny arms, arms with painted nails and bracelets, arms of Madrid or Paris; and they say the lofty tree cannot be climbed." Martí creates a picture that is the antithesis of virility: "If they are Parisians or Madrilenians, let them stroll along the Prado under the lamplights, or take sherbet at Tortoni's." With his swishy entrance and request for strawberry ice cream on the day when chocolate is served, Diego's presence transforms Copellia into Café Tortoni. While queer audiences in the West may delight in what they read as Diego's flamboyance and daring, he is arguably a culturally conservative character. As José Quiroga asserts, "In spite of all the radical pretensions Paz has given him, Diego is a profoundly conservative character not only in terms of culture but, more importantly, in his assessment of how sexual politics should be inscribed in the revolution."[20]

Fresa y chocolate was widely received as a progressive representation of gays in Cuba and to some extent as an indictment of Cuba's official policy toward gays, a policy that has included, from 1965 to 1968, sentences of forced labor at "reeducation" camps for homosexuals, the infamous UMAPs (Unidades Militares de Ayuda a la Producción). The depictions of the gay (Europeanized, effete) character and the socialist youth (masculine) character clearly fit into a postcolonial logic that situates the Cuban homosexual like Martí's Parisians and Madrilenians as white, foreign, and the "New Man" in Cuba not only as hypermasculine but also as racially hybrid—the designated stakeholder for the nation.

For example, Martí's "*mestizo autóctono*" ("autochthonic mestizo"), reinscribed as the "New Man" or socialist youth in the postrevolutionary state, requires a strictly metaphorical understanding of race that represses a history of racial domination in Cuba in order to narrativize racial mixing in positive terms and achieve a homogenous (albeit anxious) national identity. The postcolonial rhetoric of hybridity (articulated in the nineteenth-century notion of the *mestizo autóctono*), palpable to the Cuban spectator, serves the postcolonial state in managing a history of white racial domination. The figures of the gay man and the socialist youth, already encoded as Ariel/Caliban, reinforce the representation in Cuba of the homosexual as European, decadent, and treasonous; the logic of this dialectic requires absolutely that the gay character be expelled from the state at the conclusion of Gutiérrez Alea's film.

At one point in the essay, Martí, enraptured in the fervor of his own rhetoric, attests to the virile character ("*carácter viril*") of the new Americans using language that suggests male sexual excitement: "Make the natural blood of the nations course and throb through their veins! Erect, with the happy, sparkling eyes of workingmen, the new Americans salute one another from country to country."[21] Martí's America is populated by men, and ultimately, the miscegenation that produces his mestizo, in fact a metaphorical miscegenation, occurs between men. As Emilio Bejel argues, "homosexuality and homoeroticism is inscribed, by negation, in the prescriptive models of the national Cuban narrative" (16). If the male homosexual must be figured as European and alien within the Cuban narrative, he also anxiously fulfills a mediating role, negotiating Cuba's modernity in relationship to the rest of the hemisphere, whether it is the modernity of the blond nation to the north or that of a cosmopolitan Buenos Aires.

As I mention above, critics seldom mention the film's racial politics. Charles Nero provides an interesting exception. Nero critiques *Strawberry and Chocolate*'s conservative race politics, observing for instance that "[t]he film never implies that there may even be an African or African-based New World Creole model for Diego's homosexuality, despite the well-documented fact that men who have sex with other men frequently assume important roles in West African–based Creole religions in the Americas" (Nero 63). I concur with Nero's framing of the text as racial allegory. He offers a provocative interpretation of that allegory, arguing that Diego, coded as European, serves as a civilizing influence on David, whose body represents Cuba: "The elevation of Eurocentrism is important for *Fresa y chocolate*'s critique of Cuba. The film continually presents Diego's gifts of Euro-American high culture as medicinal doses and injections to rejuvenate and regenerate a body that is either ailing or stagnating. The cure for this ailing body—David's and Cuba's—is European civilization" (Nero 63–64). However, Nero does not account for a history of figuring the homosexual as Ariel. Diego's femininity undermines his critiques of the revolution. It is precisely Diego's identification with European culture that marks him as alien and treacherous. According to Nero, the representations of Diego and David also participate "in the historical practice of whitening when it privileges European culture as an antidote for an ailing Cuban body" (Nero 65). As he explains, "Diego's gifts, and David's subsequent acceptance of them, advance by whitening the racially dubious young Communist" (Nero 66). Again, I think Nero misreads the film's negotiations of Diego's Europeanized identity. However, his attention to the ideology of whitening is insightful in that the hybridity that Martí celebrates is metaphorical. David represents a Calibanic figure, following Martí, whose hybridity also circulates metaphorically within the rhetoric of Cuban nationalism. Nero's interpretation prompts us to think about how the school of

Caliban remains seduced by the very properties it condemns, including Eurocentric sensibilities and homosexuality, perhaps desirous even of that blond nation to the north whose encroachments define the borders of Martí's "Our America." Caliban and Ariel cannot be riven, despite what seems Diego's inevitable removal from the island.

Nero is not alone in reading the film allegorically. Many critics point to the proclivity for allegory in Cuban filmmaking of this era. Francine A'ness, for example, posits that "[t]his allegorizing process was used so consistently through the 1980's that it has today become a convention easily recognized by contemporary Cuban audiences, who have grown accustomed to reading narratives of the nation in their national cinema."[22] This puts an additional onus on critics to contextualize the film within Cuban history and the local realities of early 1990s Havana. As Bejel argues, "All of the main characters in *Strawberry and Chocolate* can be seen as engaged in the symbolic acts of national allegory." In that sense, the film does not read necessarily as a testament to the growing tolerance among Cuban people toward homosexuals. It may or may not. Diego's homosexuality, for instance, also represents for Cuban audiences the condition of exile: "Diego, it must be remembered, is an allegorical figure, occupying an allegorical space, and as such he is an amalgam of many traits associated with a marginal figure in Cuba—homosexual, artist, bourgeois, exile" (A'ness 95). Even among homophobic spectators in Cuba, Diego's sexuality might still represent a symbol of social protest, accounting for the broad popularity of the narrative in its various forms, from short fiction to the stage to cinema. Paul Julian Smith notes the enjoyment of a straight Cuban exile audience: "when I first saw *Strawberry and Chocolate* at an informal screening of a pirate video in New York, the mainly Cuban exile, mainly straight audience found almost every one of Diego's lines, however pathetic, hysterically funny. His plight did not provoke the sympathy Alea professes to intend."[23]

Enrico Mario Santí argues that Paz's text accrues significance during the "special period":

By 1991 Cuba was already undergoing the so-called "special period," which placed undue restraints on all cultural activity, presumably for economic reasons. It is therefore plausible that the Paz story was slowly becoming the implicit protest symbol of this period—much as the *jineteras* would do for Cuba's sexual tourism and the *balseros*, or rafters, for the regime's moral and economic failures.[24]

Santi, among others, privileges the theme of reconciliation as the film's imperative. The film engages a mode of seduction toward this reconciliation; however, it is a rather de-eroticized one. Cuban American anthropologist Ruth Behar also speaks to the film's deployment toward reconciliation: "Cinema in Cuba after the revolution became a touchstone for public discourse, and there is no question that the mutual recognition of Diego and David represents the possibility of many reconciliations, including national reconciliation between those who left and those who stayed."[25]

Those multiple reconciliations might include also, according to Nicholas Balaisis, reconciling Cuban people to the Cuban state:

> The film is seen to offer an apology on behalf of the state for the unfortunate "errors" perpetrated in the past and suggests that the revolution can be reformed from within, without the need for a change in the political status quo. From this perspective, Cuban film evidences a contradiction of the public sphere, carefully allaying doubts that citizens may feel toward the state and steering them away from political change.[26]

However, Balaisis complicates this perspective by positing the "ideological friction" of an oppositional, minority spectator. Building on the scholarship of Stephanie and James Donald, Balaisis imagines a "symbolic public sphere" available to the spectator who, responding to cues in the film, can "read the film obliquely":

While the film remains politically conservative in many ways, suggesting perhaps naively that the Cuban revolution can be reformed from within, it again shrouds this "solution" with an enigmatic silence. After all, the film concludes with Diego's self-imposed exile to the United States, an act that is conspicuously unexplained in the film, thus deferring the broader political meaning of his departure to the Cuban audience to decipher. Does he leave, for instance, because the Cuban revolution is ultimately incapable of reform? Or does he leave because he himself is not able (or willing) to persist and see through the reforms that are inevitable? Whether these questions work ultimately to shore up the base of Cuban revolutionary power, or seed more democratic alternatives is unknown, however, in both cases, the film opens up a range of important political questions available to the attuned Cuban spectator. (39–40)

The responses to *Fresa y chocolate*, which included—as with the short story—a wave of theatrical adaptations in Havana, speak to a vibrant public sphere of spectators engaging the film obliquely and perhaps oppositionally.[27]

The film also aligns Diego at once with bourgeois values and foreign interests, marking him—and arguably homosexuality—as counter-revolutionary. When Nancy protests Diego's extravagance in planning a Lezaman lunch for David, we learn that the meal will run him one hundred dollars. Especially during the "special period," the delicacies that Diego secures for the lunch also communicate to Cuban audiences his relative privilege and his probable connections to foreigners. David makes this much clear in Paz's story, when he wonders to himself about the sources for Diego's special lunch:

[S]uddenly I started to feel uneasy, because though enjoying the lunch I couldn't help some nerve ends remaining raw in that feast, on red alert, spectating, concluding that the lobsters, prawns, Lübeck asparagus and grapes must have been bought in the special shops for diplomats and consequently were proof of his relationship with foreigners, which, in my role as a special agent, I should communicate to the comrade who was yet to become my Ismael. (61)

Building on these suspicions, in ways both tacit and explicit, the film arguably works to undermine the sympathies "special period" Cuban audiences might extend to Diego. At the very least, the same cosmopolitanism that endeared Diego to Anglo American spectators complicates the sympathies of Cuban spectators.

I don't want to discount the impact of the film for gay Cubans. Ian Lumsden argues that the "production and distribution of *Fresa y chocolate* was a landmark for Cuban gays. It unleashed a popular discourse about a culturally tabooed and politically repressed issue that went beyond the confines of the film itself" (Lumsden 194). I also don't want to overestimate its impact. The film was not as broadly seen across the island as people believe, and it did not air on television in Cuba until 2008, a full fifteen years after its release.[28] The degree to which *Strawberry and Chocolate* shifted cultural attitudes across the island remains negligible. Ricardo Ortiz is among the film's more skeptical critics:

> While the open discussions of the value of homosexual citizens to the Revolution in both the film and the story reflect a relaxation of policies and attitudes toward homosexuals in Cuba, the discourse of the "New" Revolutionary "Man" or citizen is now as old as the 1959 Revolution itself, when it cropped up already indebted to an even older Stalinist ideal. Unfortunately, neither Paz's book nor Gutiérrez's film suggests that the concept of the "New Man" is any closer to abandoning the values of hypermasculine stoicism and toughness celebrated in the Soviet Union in the 1940's. ("Docile Bodies," 91)

Yet this revolutionary "New Man," if we also trace his Cuban lineage back to the foundational text of Martí's "Our America," reveals a masculinity set in crisis. Despite how vigorously the Cuban state has in the past worked to expel the likes of Diego from the country, his troubling desires haunt the nation. (Unlike Ortiz, I do think the Paz book introduces some interesting ambiguity around the New Man's sexuality, while the film betrays a masculinist—and nationalist—anxiety ultimately less challenging to the status quo.)

Universalizing from his own experience, the gay cosmopolitan spectator projects himself into the life of another nation, displacing and obscuring local histories. The multitude of theatrical adaptations in Havana speaks to complex and sundry local engagements with the film and the story that are beyond the scope of this chapter. But certainly that multiplicity tells us it is important to disrupt the colonizing appetite of North American and Northwest European gay spectators eager to violently recognize themselves in others through the configuration of a queer globality. It is critical to think too about exactly how and to what ends films like *Fresa y chocolate* seduce the gay cosmopolitan.

4

You Can Have My Brown Body and Eat It, Too!

They say when trouble comes close ranks, and so the white
people did.
—Jean Rhys, *Wide Sargasso Sea*

The Gay Shame conference held at the University of Michigan in 2003
was a turning point for me. As a panelist on the closing roundtable, I pro-
tested the unacknowledged centering of white gay male experience that
pervaded conceptualizations of gay shame as well as a spectacularization
of racial difference that had worked violently, I argued, to consolidate
the community of whiteness at the conference. My comments polarized
the audience, prompting some further criticisms of the conference but
also a retrenchment of white identity politics, particularly among white
gay men. Regardless of how I articulated my critique at Gay Shame, I was
heard—or so it seemed to me—by significant portions of the audience
not only to be assuming a position against pornography but also a stance
against pleasure itself. I could write this off as the result of ineloquence
on my part, intransigence on the part of a particular audience (chiefly
gay white male academics), or both. Alternatively, I can look back at that
unpleasant afternoon now twelve years ago as a moment of telling and
perhaps even productive tension. Reflecting back on the conference, I
suspect that ineloquence and intransigence were both operating more
generally in ways that derailed possibilities for conversation. However, I
imagine the exchange would not proceed any more productively today.

Queer theory is very particular about the kinds of trouble with which
it troubles itself. The problem of race in particular presents queer theory
with dilemmas over which it actively untroubles itself. I speculate in
this chapter on the resistance within establishmentarian queer theory

to thinking race critically, a resistance that habitually classifies almost any form of race studies as a retreat into identity politics. This defensive posture helps entrench institutionally the transparent white subject characteristic of so much queer theorizing. Queer theorists who can invoke that transparent subject, and choose to do so, reap the dividends of whiteness.[1]

In addition to marking an inside and out of queer theory, I further elaborate with this chapter a demystification of the primitive or "brown" body commodified by dominant gay male culture. I consider that brown body as axial to the formation of a cosmopolitan gay male identity and community. More specifically, I argue that this brown body mediates gay male shame. These speculations are prompted by my confrontation with queer theory at the Gay Shame conference at the University of Michigan, March 27–29, 2003. The location and date are significant to situating this conference historically, especially for a discussion of identity politics in higher education. Gay Shame occurred within a week of the U.S. invasion of Iraq and in the midst of the *Grutter v. Bollinger* (2003) and *Gratz v. Bollinger* (2003) affirmative action cases involving the University of Michigan.

I was invited to participate in the conference after contacting its organizers and expressing my interest as someone working on the relationship between shame and racial embodiment. Upon arriving at Ann Arbor, I was startled to learn that of the approximately forty guests, I was the only invited queer person of color present. (Samuel Delany had been invited but canceled.) Although women of color students, faculty, and staff attended the proceedings, no persons of color from outside the university were invited as guest speakers. The schedule included some of the most prominent names in queer theory, making the absence of the many scholars of color publishing important work on race and sexuality that much more striking. Events included a screening of Andy Warhol's *Screen Test #2* (starring Mario Montez); a performance by Vaginal Davis, "Intimacy & Tomorrow"; remarks on the topic of gay shame by the conference's organizers, David Halperin and Valerie

Traub; and a discussion with Douglas Crimp about his reading of the Warhol film. Mario Montez, a Puerto Rican drag queen also featured in films by Jack Smith, and Davis, a black performance/conceptual artist and self-proclaimed "ghetto androgenue," provided the conference with what I argue constitute the prerequisite "brown" bodies for prevailing recuperations of gay shame.[2] They embodied Gay Shame's imagined prehistory. While Davis's performances may disrupt such objectifications, I do not include her as one of the queer of color invited speakers theorizing gay shame because she was not presented as such. "Intimacy & Tomorrow" was scheduled at 9:00 p.m. on March 27, following a champagne reception and the Warhol screening. Since the conference was billed as a two-day event, it is safe to presume that *Screen Test #2* and "Intimacy & Tomorrow" were not scheduled as part of the conference proceedings proper, which occurred on March 28 and 29. Warhol's work was attended to by Douglas Crimp during the opening discussion on Friday, March 28. No such discussion was scheduled to address Davis's performance, despite the prominent critical attention to her work by José Muñoz.

A distressing racialized division of labor resulted at Gay Shame. White folks performed the intellectual labor while black and brown folks just plain performed, evidently constituting the spectacle of gay shame. While race consciousness continues to function as the false consciousness of establishmentarian queer theory, I argue in this chapter that race makes all the difference for Gay Shame—its eponymous first international conference, its prevailing theoretical formulations, its primal scenes. A great deal of queer theorizing has sought to displace identity politics with an alternative anti-identitarian model, often—and perhaps disingenuously—christened "the politics of difference." This model accommodates familiar habits of the university's ideal bourgeois subject, among them his imperial gaze, his universalism, and his claims to a race-neutral objectivity. It is not surprising then to find buried underneath the boot of this establishmentarian anti-identity all sorts of dissident bodies.

In her article "Against Proper Objects" (1997), Judith Butler revisited an earlier collaboration with Biddy Martin. Asked to edit a special issue of the journal *Diacritics* dedicated to gay and lesbian studies, in 1994 Butler and Martin had "broadened the scope of that request to include work that interrogates the problem of cross-identification within and across race and postcolonial studies, gender theory, and theories of sexuality."[3] Assessing three years later this critical challenge, Butler determined that queer theory had resisted the call for boundary crossings that she and Martin had first put forth in 1994. Echoing the concerns originally voiced in Martin's essay "Sexualities without Gender," Butler expressed alarm over queer theory's wholesale transition from gender to sexuality as the proper object of its analysis. The shift from gender to sexuality does not effectively anticipate how institutionalized patriarchy and racism might be retrenched precisely as a result of this transition.

Informed at Gay Shame—and reminded several times since then—that criticisms identical to mine have recurred for over a decade, I find it instructive to revisit this earlier writing on queer theory's negotiations of identity. The interrogation into cross-identifications proposed by Martin and Butler remained unrealized nearly a decade later at Gay Shame; the resistance to such interrogations strikes me as fairly symptomatic of the present state of queer theorizing in its institutionalized forms. I share Biddy Martin's faith in the potential of queer theory to complicate questions of identity and power, but I also wish to pursue her argument that queer theorizing derails that potential by conceiving both gender and race in terms of a "fixity and miring" that provide the ground for a figural and performative sexuality.[4]

I interrogate in this chapter the cross-identifications specifically occasioned by Gay Shame to set in relief the often transparent alignments of queer theory with systemic racial domination and violence. However, I also revisit queer theory's promise to "complicate assumptions about routes of identification and desire,"[5] inspired by Butler's and Martin's still-pressing, even if long-expired, solicitation. The brown body's mediations of shame, queer theorizing, and gay male cosmopolitanism provide the cross-identifications on which I focus. My own body included, the brownness contested at Gay Shame comprised a further episode in the overdetermined black/white opposition that characterizes U.S. histories of racialization. The work of critical race theory, and in particular Cheryl Harris's essay "Whiteness as Property," charts the convergence of U.S. racial formation with property rights and the doctrines of liberalism. Harris argues that an unacknowledged "property interest in whiteness . . . forms the background against which legal disputes are framed. . . . Through this entangled relationship between race and property, historical forms of domination have evolved to reproduce subordination in the present."[6] I examine in this chapter how the brown body marks yet another evolution of this entanglement. At Gay Shame, brown bodies were allowed "access"—if it can be called that—only as spectacle for the consumption of gay cosmopolitanism.

Queer Patriot Acts

In the weeks following the Michigan fiasco, a number of allies reported to me hearing complaints that Gay Shame had been "hijacked by identitarian politics"—that Gay Shame in fact had been a great conference until its hijacking. Needless to say, I found this language staggering, especially the use of the word "hijacked." My anger at the conference resurfaced. But I was grateful, too, for how perfectly the phrase "hijacked by identitarian politics" condensed for me the political dynamics of establishmentarian queer theory. In the era of the "war on terrorism" and the USA PATRIOT Act,[7] the word "hijacked" invokes the rhetoric of national belonging—and not belonging. The restriction of brown bodies from queer theory's institutional spaces shares ideological underpinnings with the expulsion of brown bodies from the nation-state.

The PATRIOT Act demonstrates how dissidence is stigmatized onto bodies. The very presence of dissident bodies—or rather the unacceptable metaphysics of this presence as distinguished from objectification as spectacle—also constitutes a hijacking. Brown bodies must never improvise on their brownness. Whiteness experiences such improvisations as the theft of something very dear: its universal property claim to the uniqueness of being. Queer theorizing, as it has been institutionalized, is proper to—and property to—white bodies. Colored folk perform affect but can never theorize it. Actually, shame seemed strangely disaffected at the conference; U.S. race discourse stipulates that gay shame, as an experience both visceral and self-reflexive, be recuperated for whiteness. The charge of "hijacking" contains my dissent as fanaticism. But it also foregrounds queer theory's own indivisibilities—its own unacknowledged stakes in identity. Those stakes not only include whiteness, masculinity, and even heteronormativity but perhaps also do so in uniquely American formations. The queer establishment's desires and identifications align not-so-queerly with those of U.S. nationalism.

The queer theorizing of shame has invoked gay cosmopolitanism. In denaturalizing the relationship of sexuality to gender and sex, queer theory consistently locates the constitutive scenes of this disjuncture in the past. The function of shame in the formation of queer identities, for instance, is restricted primarily to childhood or to an era before Gay Pride. In so doing, queer theory also predominantly situates shame as a resistance and in opposition to normalization. At Gay Shame, for example, this primal past included the "New York City queer culture of the 1960s" (Crimp 58). This designated period of prenormalization is idealized as precivilized, but queer theory must then recruit the brown body to authenticate the scene as primitive. Gay cosmopolitanism and a complementary species of queer theorizing evolve from this shared ground. The relationship of shame to identity formation is not theorized as an ongoing, dynamic process. In fact, much queer theorizing of shame is oddly nostalgic without consideration of the dynamic, affective quality of that nostalgia. The accordingly disaffective character of gay shame reveals a formulation of "queer" indivisible from dominant white masculinity.

The abolition of the draft in 1973, despite ongoing U.S. militarism, saved the nation's white elite by sacrificing its black, brown, and poor white populations. Gay Shame's absent black and brown bodies constitute queer theory's missing in action—quite literally. The white presence at Gay Shame was conditioned literally on black and brown absence. The intellectual capacity of whiteness required the both literal and figurative presence-in-absence of the brown body as spectacle. Gay Shame's resistance, then, to thinking race needs to be understood within the context of the military's ever-browning "warrior caste" and the continuing siege on affirmative action.[8] Queer theorizing also needs to more critically regard historical criminalizations of race.[9]

In its institutionalization as an academic discipline, queer theory took the question of its political viability off the table. But if queer is to remain an effective troubling of the normative and its attendant regimes, it must painstakingly excavate its own entrenchments in normativity. Establishmentarian queer theory houses itself not only in the academy but also within the identificatory boundaries of U.S. nationalism. The shaming of brown bodies is fundamental to dominant U.S. cultures, among them now a dominant queer culture.

Why the Boys Are Always Browner on the Other Side of the Fence

What color is brown? In regard to race classification, brown is no more a natural color than black or white or yellow or red; brown is a verb.[10] "Brown" designates a kind of constitutive ambiguity within U.S. racial formations—an identity that both complicates and preserves the binary opposition white/other.[11] I use the category here to mark a position of essential itinerancy relative to naturalized, positivist classes such as white, black, Asian. Itself provisional as an identity category (a waiting station of sorts between white and black, or white and Asian, for example), I make use of "brown" provisionally myself—and tactically—to demystify how bodies are situated outside white/black or white/Asian binaries to consolidate cosmopolitan, first world identities. As a repository for the disowned, projected desires of a cosmopolitan subject, it is alternately (or simultaneously) primitive, exotic, savage, pansexual, and abject. It is black and not black, Asian and not Asian, white and not white. In an age of weak multiculturalism, it is what it needs to be to maintain existing racial hierarchies, a race discourse morally divested from politics and social redistribution. That ambiguity designated here as "brown" is opportunistically and systemically deployed at times of crisis—as instanced by the intensified race profiling authorized by 9/11.[12]

Examining how "brown" circulates within a cosmopolitan gay male sexual economy proves worthwhile critically for reconstructing the racialized character of all sexuality and for chipping away at the curiously harmonious race discourses of the Right and the Left, namely, color blindness and anti-identity. These approaches to thinking and, more significantly, delegislating race constitute perhaps a common discourse rather than analogous ones. In this project, I have used "brown" to trouble the poststructuralist critiques of identity politics that participate in retrenching white patriarchal order and dismantling the hugely significant yet still-inadequate gains made since, ironically, *Brown v. Board of Education* (1954). Having celebrated its fiftieth anniversary the year after Gay Shame, the *Brown* decision—located historically as an inauguration of the civil rights era—looms large over this project in the wake of the Bollinger cases, the demographic transformation of the military witnessed by the brown warrior caste dispatched onto (or sacrificed in) Iraq, and state actions punitively directed at expelling immigrants from the domain of civil society and its nominal protections.

I have used the word "cosmopolitan" to identify a subject position originating with a white, urban, leisure-class gay male whose desire is cast materially onto the globe at the close of the nineteenth century. A range of mobilities, transformed or generated by industrialization (i.e., class privilege, whiteness, transportation technology, mass media, tourism) and, eventually, postindustrial society (i.e., communications and information technologies) provide conditions for a cosmopolitan gay male subject. However, that subject need not materially possess the full range of these mobilities. He can occupy an ambivalent position as both exoticizing/exotic and subject/object in relation to a cosmopolitan gay male desire. His experience of this subjectification can be simultaneously resistant and ecstatic. Although originating with a white leisure class, this gay cosmopolitanism is by no means in its contemporary manifestations limited to white or urban or affluent subjects. It constitutes a major rite of gay male acculturation. Gay men of color participate in these contradictions but do not emerge unscathed. The desires comprising the cosmopolitan gay male subject in fact reinscribe oppressive racial hierarchies while enjoining gay men of color to both authenticate and celebrate those desires and the sexual cultures they organize. After all, the culture of the gay male cosmopolitan follows his desire and necessarily embroils the objects of that desire. If his desire is cast materially onto the world, so too is the culture that accommodates that desire. The development of an Anglo American tourism industry to service a growing leisure class contributed to the formation of a cosmopolitan gay male identity, making available for consumption both spaces and bodies imagined as precivilized. The very notion of civilization requires a fantasied, primitive space onto which repressed desires are projected and disavowed. This idyllic space, populated by pansexual, uninhibited brown bodies—bodies without shame—promised liberation from Victorian restrictions on same-sex desires. These characteristics—mobility and shame and fantasies about the primitive—continue to shape dominant Anglo American gay male culture.

The tourism scholar Howard Hughes's observation that "tourism and being gay are inextricably linked" functions for me here as a kind of axiom.[13] Being gay always involves, to some extent, being someplace else. Just to be clear, I am not talking about same-sex desire or even practices, which can be satisfied even in the most fixed and isolated of conditions and which do not in themselves necessarily signal any kind of group identification. Neither am I using "gay" as an ahistorical, universal category.

In reference to Hughes's formulation, I understand "gay" as an already universalizing agent or its trace subject. Identification as "gay" is premised on mobility. Whether in the South Seas of William Stoddard's Victorian travel writing or New York City's Chelsea or anywhere other than the heteronormative confines of the traditionally defined "home" and "family," being "gay" requires some kind of travel, actual or imagined. The most canonical expression of being gay, "coming out of the closet," is a quintessential articulation of the link between identity and travel. Needless to say, the mobility that modern gay identity requires is not universally available. Here we encounter trouble in the form of noncanonical bodies (not surprisingly, also quite often brown bodies) nonetheless interpellated as gay—gays who cannot properly be gay. The closet, as the primary cultural canon of mainstream gay and lesbian politics, is a spatial metaphor, yet there is insufficient consideration of how that figurative space presupposes specific material conditions. The closet metaphor spatially and temporally suggests access to privacy not collectively experienced by all sexual minorities. The privacy this metaphor takes for granted requires specific economic, cultural, and familial circumstances. Likewise, the "coming out" metaphor suggests a kind of mobility not universally available. These canonized metaphors for gay and lesbian experience crystallize homosexual identity within a tradition of possessive individualism. Coming out promises liberation and celebrates a species of individualism in the form of self-determination. Conceptually and materially, that freedom and self-determination are premised on the property of whiteness. The closet narrativizes gay and lesbian identity in a manner that violently excludes or includes the subjects it names according to their access to specific kinds of privacy, property, and mobility.

For Jasbir Puar, as well as Hughes, the link between travel and a specifically gay identity is also determined by homophobia. Much of the writing on gay and lesbian travel narrativizes this movement primarily as a kind of dislocation (a flight from oppression to freedom) without adequately examining how such movement also constitutes an exercise in mobility and privilege. In her article on queer mobility, Puar departs from the dominant paradigms in tourism studies, shifting her focus onto a theorization of gay and lesbian consumption. As an example of the traditional approach to understanding gay and lesbian travel, she quotes Thomas Roth, a marketing strategist whose surveys are used by the gay and lesbian tourism industry: "Many [tourists] are closeted, or come from repressive families, communities or societies. At least during our vacations, we should be free to be ourselves in a welcoming environment."[14]

What kinds of violences are necessary to consolidate the constituency designated by the pronoun "we"? Roth makes it clear that the freedom "to be ourselves" requires the securing of a space. His use of the pronoun "ourselves" signals the possessiveness of his subject, but the grammar suppresses the acquisitiveness that the subject "we" must exercise to obtain and safeguard the possessive individuality coordinated by the infinitive phrase "to be ourselves." The mobility of Roth's touristing subject is enabled by privileges of class, race, citizenship, and quite often also gender (hence the need to also distinguish between cosmopolitan gay and lesbian mobilities). Roth's gay travelers move not only from the domestic/repressive to the foreign/liberating but also from isolation to publicity and, arguably, from obscurity to identity. "We" exist so long as "we" can freely consume abroad the pleasure that both defines and defiles us at home. Coming out of the closet, the canonized narrative for gay and lesbian identity, hinges on mobility, a globalized consumerism, and imperialism.

Before they can be deemed "welcoming," the "environments" Roth so vaguely references must be properly colonized to satisfy the desires of gay and lesbian cosmopolitans. This is true not only for the international locations of gay and lesbian tourism but also for the domestic locations of gay and lesbian gentrification. The formation of these identities, and I focus here on the gay male cosmopolitan, demands spaces imagined as precivilized. The cosmopolitan calls upon the native bodies to authenticate the underdevelopment (in every sense) and innocence of these "welcoming" destinations. Puar points out that "on the one hand, there is the disruption of heterosexual space and, on the other, the use of the exotic to transgress; in this case, the exotic is signaled by discourses of homophobia."[15] This fantasy of the exotic is necessary to the formation of a modern gay male cosmopolitan identity. Queer theorizing more resolutely needs to investigate how dominant Euro-American formations of gay, lesbian, and queer cultures (not only during this era of normalization but also historically) collude with a hegemonic white masculinity.

Speaking in Tongues without Even Trying

Speaking as a member of the conference's "final discussion," stationed before an assembled vanguard of queer theorizing (which I identified at the time, vis-à-vis my own generically brown condition, as a Queer Illuminati), I could not help but realize that I too was obliging Gay Shame's desire for brown spectacle. The circumstance was a familiar one: a scholarly presentation deteriorates into what feels like a cake walk, and I am left pondering the futility of any intervention on my part. I was there neither to comprise nor to interrogate the category "queer"; I was there to bind its community.

For a conference devoted to theorizing shame, there was curiously little scholarship specifically addressing affect. Despite the conference theme, the proceedings reproduced an opposition between theory and affect, particularly in its gendered and raced foundations, characteristic of Enlightenment thought: theory is to affect as masculine is to feminine; civilized to primitive; rational to paranoid; white to other. The brown thug and the sentimental feminine find themselves unlikely compatriots in this opposition. The identities "gay" or "queer" or "lesbian" do not preempt queer theorists from reinstituting masculinist biases and patriarchal privileges. The most elitist manifestations of theorizing, even when articulated by queer subjects, also often evidence the most vulgar masculinisms.[16]

Having been accused at the conference of practicing "paranoid criticism" and being too literal,[17] I provisionally maintain my guilt on both counts and inhabit that paranoia to license here the following rhetorical indulgence: Everything I am about to say in this essay has already been said. I make this concession on behalf of a particular kind of resistant reader. Namely, I have in mind readers who might feel disgruntled about hearing "the same thing" for the past ten or even twenty years, a protest voiced by conference participants at Ann Arbor.

Rather than focusing on a critique's "originality," queer theory is better served by interrogating its own capacity to listen imaginatively. The professional pressure to produce "originality" is really a call to make property claims demarcating intellectual territory and thus an appeal to privatism and individualism. It is entirely possible that I am revisiting already exhausted arguments, but it is also possible that queer theory quite opportunely resists engaging particular types of inquiry. The field needs to ascertain how any such resistance is rewarded. After a decade (or longer) of hearing "the same thing," it might be time for queer theory to start listening. The chronic failure of establishmentarian queer theory to revisit its fundamental collusions with American liberalism consolidates indivisibilities—white, patriarchal, heteronormative—contrary to any professed anti-identity. This refusal to engage race consciousness corresponds exactly to the historical contingency of property rights on U.S. racial oppression.

There is little consideration within establishmentarian queer theory as to whether it has at all toppled the exclusionary infrastructures of the spaces it inherits. Indeed, the space queer theory occupies within the academy, it has inherited from liberal humanism and its contemporary multiculturalist traditions. It is neither defeatist nor simplistically nihilistic to concede that queer theory is necessarily compromised at the junctures of institutionalization, nationalism, and citizenship; queer theorists might in fact approach this bind productively. By interrogating the complicity demanded by institutionalization, we can more effectively resist such collusion and attempt to reinvent our relationships to the academy and perhaps even transform the institution itself.

How Do You Solve a Problem Like "Poor Mario"?

Douglas Crimp's "Mario Montez, For Shame," originally published in a collection of critical revaluations of Eve Sedgwick's contributions to critical theory, provided a critical foundation for the conference. In arguing for a productive (or ethical) mobilization of gay shame, Crimp invokes Sedgwick's oft-reiterated axiom, "People are different from each other." He gleans from this axiom "the ethical necessity of developing ever finer tools for encountering, upholding, and valuing other's differences—or better, differences and singularities—nonce-taxonomies, as she wonderfully names such tools."[18] However, both Crimp's essay and the conference proceedings demonstrate a resistance within queer theory to appreciating how racial differences contribute to queer singularities. Such resistance, hardly ethical or productive, secures both white privilege and its transparency, and forecloses the rigorous examinations of desire and fantasy and pleasure that we should expect from queer theory.

Crimp's essay focuses on what he reads as Andy Warhol's and Ronnie Tavel's humiliation of Mario Montez, a Puerto Rican drag queen starring in Warhol's *Screen Test #2*. Trusting Warhol to speak for Montez, who remains entirely passive in relationship to both queer and U.S. cultures, Crimp renders Montez supplemental to the "New York City queer culture of the 1960s" that Crimp's project seeks to reclaim. Montez forms a surface for the inscription of that culture but is never a participant. His presence at the scene of the crime—whether that be the 1960s experimentation of Warhol's Factory or the 2003 Gay Shame of Ann Arbor—is incidental. The categories "Puerto Rican" and "Catholic," deployed monolithically, comprise for Crimp the totality of Montez's difference. Crimp interrogates neither Warhol's nor his own investments in the particularities of this representation of difference. His unqualified confidence in a second-hand account of Montez's Catholicism together with generalizations about Puerto Rican national culture provide Crimp with the only tools he needs to construct a narrative for Montez's shame.

The absence, for example, of any examination of Warhol's Catholicism is only one of several telling omissions in Crimp's project.

For Crimp, only Warhol and Tavel can exercise agency. Crimp's reading of *Screen Test #2* elides any possible authority and oppositionality on the part of Montez: "Poor Mario looks alternately bewildered and terrified" (62). Montez is always authentically authentic. In response to Tavel's mocking, according to Crimp, Montez is "so delighted as to make it obvious he's still hoodwinked" (61). Conversely, Warhol's and Tavel's insight and irony become authentic qualities. Warhol, for example, demonstrates an "uncanny ability to conceal dead-on insight in the bland, unknowing remark" (59). Warhol is unknowing and insightful, mindful even when unmindful, in opposition to Montez's alternate bewilderment and terror in the face of authority.

Crimp identifies "exposure" as the subject of *Screen Test #2*. He cites Stefan Brecht's celebration of Warhol's genius: "Here again Warhol's true genius for abstraction paid off: he invented a camera-technique that was nothing but exposure" (59). I concur with Crimp that "exposure" is a subject of the film. The object of that exposure, however, is not fixed; as Crimp acknowledges, the film's deployment of shame exposes him, too. Exposure can never be equivalent to just one thing; it requires at least two actors (curator and spectator) and an object. Perhaps what is masterful about *Screen Test #2* is its unfixing of the components of exposure. In other words, what is masterful about the film is its undetermined mastery. Crimp imagines Montez only as the object of exposure. But what if authority in the film is reassigned? The moments that Crimp reads as "bewilderment and terror" might also comprise Montez's pirating (hijacking?) of authority. Montez shifts the film's scrutiny (its defining quality, according to Crimp and Brecht) alternately onto Warhol, Tavel, the spectator.

For Crimp the important questions are as follows: "How might we square these scenes of violation and shaming with what I'm describing as an ethical project of giving visibility—and I want also to say dignity—to a queer world of differences and singularities in the 1960s?

What does the viewer's discomfiture at Warhol's techniques of exposure do to the usual processes of spectator identifications?" (63). Crimp's questions generate several of my own: what violences are imposed on Mario Montez and similarly situated subjects by the visibility Crimp seeks to confer? What does it mean for Montez (or a subject similarly situated) that his exposure is a necessary condition for conferring dignity on others? (What of Montez's dignity?) Who is this isolated viewer by whose discomfiture all other spectator identifications are measured?

The ethico-political possibilities inherent in shame emerge from the urgent yet impossible dissociation upon which it insists. Crimp explains, "In the act of taking on the shame that is properly someone else's, I simultaneously feel my utter separateness from even that person. . . . I do not share the other's identity. I simply adopt the other's vulnerability to being shamed. . . . [T]he other's difference is preserved; it is not claimed as my own" (65). The problem with Crimp's formulation is that the other's shame is already always his own before it can be "properly someone else's." The only shame Crimp takes on is the shame he projects onto Montez. The urgency to dissociate from the other's shamed body arises subsequent to his vexed assimilation of that body. Montez's body is a palate for Crimp's shame (as it is in different contexts for my own).

Perhaps the clearest evidence of Crimp's identification with (and incorporation of) Montez is his continued reference to the actor by his first name, while he refers to Tavel and Warhol exclusively by their surnames. He forecloses any possibility that Montez might also actively coauthor the text rather than merely serve as its passive object. Crimp cites an anecdote from *POPism* in which Warhol describes how "poor Mario Montez got his feelings hurt for real in his scene" while shooting "Chelsea Girls" (58). This description defines for Crimp Montez's relationship to exposition and ultimately to (gay white male) shame. Montez feels for real while Warhol fictionalizes, experiments, creates, and Crimp expounds. As Biddy Martin forecast a decade ago, the "fixity and miring" (105) of race and gender provide the ground for queer theory's performative sexuality.

If You White, You Right; If You Black, Get Back; If You Brown . . .
Prepare to Get Your Spectacle On!

The reduction to spectacle, a reduction to the body, was most devastatingly realized in a presentation on Plato's *Symposium* late in the conference's first day. As Ellis Hanson addressed Plato, Derrida, the "cadaverization" of the teacher's body, and hypothesized that love is a victimless crime, images of a model named Kiko, featured in *Latin Inches* magazine, flashed behind him. These publicity photos for the video *Learning Latin* (1996) show Kiko, costumed in something akin to a colonial schoolboy uniform (khaki shorts, white polo shirt), posing in a classroom. He appears in various states of undress, at first with his dick hanging out of his unzipped fly, eventually bent naked over a stool. On the blackboard behind him, the sentence "I love sex" has been written over and over, as Kiko has apparently been kept after class, and this is his punishment. During his presentation, Hanson wore a uniform identical to the one worn by Kiko, suggesting a kind of mimetic annihilation, the nostalgia characteristic of the queer theorizing of shame, in this instance a colonial nostalgia. At no point did Hanson offer a substantive reading of the images flashing behind him.[19]

The presentation rendered me speechless. Initially, I attributed that speechlessness to exhaustion. Later I determined that my speechlessness might be more productively understood as a quality of collective trauma.[20] It is useful to think about the experience of racial oppression as a kind of trauma, to think about how shame and trauma might somehow be constitutive of race. Trauma results not only from a "discrete happening" but also, as Kai Erikson argues, from a *"constellation of life experiences . . . from a persisting condition* as well as from an acute event."[21] This definition broadens the understanding of trauma so that it is not isolated to discrete experiences and personalities; trauma can also function as a constitutive social force in relation to group identity. Erikson clarifies how trauma might generate communality: "Traumatic wounds inflicted on individuals can combine to create a mood, an ethos—a group culture, almost—that is different from (and more than) the sum of the private wounds that make it up. Trauma, that is, has a social dimension" (185).

I experienced the Kiko presentation (and ultimately the Gay Shame conference in its entirety) as a kind of assault. Not an assault in the sense that Ellis Hanson intended to hurt me or anybody else (although neither would I categorize his presentation, or his desire, or any desire, as innocent), but an assault in the sense that the images displayed have a context and a history that are meaningful to me in ways very different from the way they are meaningful, I suspect, for Hanson. These images, or more precisely the politics of their display, belong for me to an already existing "constellation of life experiences." My hope that queer theory might learn to listen more imaginatively finds a prescription in the questions Erikson introduces to trauma theory: "To what extent may one conclude that the communal dimension of trauma is one of its distinctive clinical signatures? And to what extent does it make sense to conclude that the traumatized view of the world conveys a wisdom that ought to be heard?" (198), an affect requiring recognition?

The first comment after Hanson's presentation came from Tobin Siebers, seated next to me. Siebers, a disability studies theorist, jokingly announced that Kiko's was the most "able-bodied dick" he'd ever seen. I felt kicked in the gut. Can the reduction—not just to body, but to dick—find any more unequivocal articulation? Yet if I cannot convey to fellow queer theorists how this whole scene constituted for me an assault, and if they cannot hear my criticism, how can I be sure that I am ever intelligible to them as human? Following Siebers's remark, the next few comments also joked, albeit nervously, about the photos. I listened dumbfounded as Hanson was teased about him and Plato having to compete with the big, "purple" dick (the biggest anyone had ever seen, it turns out) for the audience's attention. There occurred no substantive discussion about the representation of Kiko, about fantasy, about racialized desire, or even about Hanson's reading of Plato. Kiko's dick assumed its historical place as the focal point of white fantasy.

That night and into the next day I heard several queer theorists, white men and women, proclaim that Kiko's was indeed the biggest dick they had ever seen—an astonishing declaration from queer theorists, many of whom write on gay male pornography. I guarantee that this was not the biggest dick conference participants had ever seen; a few seconds on the Internet would turn up innumerable dicks fatter and longer. The need even to explain this is demeaning. But the circumstance is indicative also of dominant-culture fantasies about black male sexuality. Kiko is both Latino and black. I cannot be certain that he would identify himself as black. Maybe he would; maybe he would not. (The complications of the classification "Latino" are a topic for another essay.)

This incident demonstrates, however, how the brown body signifies ambiguities that ultimately reinforce contemporary white hegemony through its intersection with a spectralized blackness. Kiko's brownness removes his body from the history of white predations on the black male body, in particular the black male body that emerged after Reconstruction: the "free" black man ruled by savage and insatiable sexual appetites. This unremitting cultural fixation on the black penis needs to be understood as a legacy of lynching. The transformation of the black penis into a magic object requires that the racial-sexual violence become naturalized; in other words, the castrated penis must itself become fantastic in order to sanction genocidal violence. The culture of lynching continues to generate fresh enactments of its ritual violence: the separation of the man from the penis, the substitution of penis for the man, the impossibility of a "private" black sexuality, contempt for black humanity. His sexual voraciousness is located in his mythically proportioned manhood, the product of a white imagination that seeks to exterminate the black man for more reasons than it can ever allow itself to name. This white desire for a black male body, alternately manifested as love, disgust, fear, and murderousness, resides at the heart of U.S. sexual cultures, straight and queer.

The brownness conferred on Kiko when he is designated as "Latin" (itself an already ambiguous sign) circumvents troubling histories of racial oppression that are more immediate to the white imagination in the form of enslavement, lynching, and police brutality. Already forgetful about its history of state-sanctioned white-on-black violence, the United States remains blissfully amnesiac about its violent imperial history. The ambiguities of brownness function to unburden fantasies of black sexuality from their troubling histories; those same fantasies, and new ones, may be revisited on the brown body. In other words, one manifestation of the brown body occurs in the form of a black body un*moor*ed, if you will, from material history and fixed instead to the landscape of a gay cosmopolitan imagination.

Kiko's dick was the biggest anyone had ever seen because it was that same mythic black dick dreamed by white desire, except for being transported to a location where desires are not so burdened by troubling histories, like those recounted in Baldwin's story of lynching. Gay shame's desire for Kiko seeks to humiliate Kiko, to symbolically annihilate him, but in order to mistranslate its own murderous desire as love, it must locate Kiko at the limits of civilization, where he is beautifully abject, where he is brown and shameless. Cosmopolitan gay male subjectivity is founded on the humiliation of "brown" primitives and thugs, a humiliation often subsequently misnamed as "love."

Kiko became brown within the contact zones of desire. His brownness functions in itself as a kind of traveling contact zone; it entertains all sorts of fantasies of the primitive. The brown body is a fetish for what the cosmopolitan has lost or forgotten at the other side (the brown underside) of civilization. Kiko is browned by the symbols that converge at his (and Gay Shame's) horizon: the moniker "Latin Inches"; the colonial schoolboy uniform; the nickname; his banjee-ness; his accessibility as spectacle. Once available to cosmopolitan consumption, the brown body generates desire, but only insofar as it is the location where different stories of desire become possible. The brown body's ambiguity is endlessly generative. It provides cosmopolitan gay male subjects with objects of desire and with the super-abundant raw material from which to compose the story of that desire. The ambiguity of brownness contra the prevailing black/white opposition of U.S. race discourse secures for the contemporary cosmopolitan gay male a location in which he can materially and psychically flex his desire with impunity. He gets to have his brown body and eat it, too.

Dismissed as identity politics and a crude appeal to personal experience, my attempt to communicate the indignity and assault I experienced at the conference could not be heard. I propose that the resistance I confronted, articulated via poststructuralist critiques of identity, designates the need for white dominant culture to sustain the impossibility of a private black sexuality. The mythology of the black penis remains too deep-rooted in the popular imagination for me to convince the cockstruck attendees at Gay Shame that Kiko's privates were not the biggest they had ever seen. Euphemisms aside, Kiko's "privates" were not in any sense private, either. I did not advance an antipornography position at the conference, but I suspect that the defensiveness on the part of many queer theorists present, especially among the gay white men, resulted from an overdetermined misreading of my comments as just that. For example, one respondent insisted that I had contended in my remarks that he (a white man) "could not look at" nude images of Kiko. He perceived my criticism as a competing property claim on Kiko's body.

I was not there to make any such property claim, but it was made emphatically clear to me, by Hanson's presentation as well as by the reaction to my comments, that I am most certainly not entitled to do so. For the cosmopolitan gay male subject, the brown body constitutes communal property. As a site of communion for whiteness, the brown body realizes white indivisibility. My inquiry into the semantics of Kiko's body constituted a trespass. It represented for white desire an exercise of acquisitiveness on my part that is proper only to whiteness. To pose the question of the semantics of the brown body is to take meaning from the fetish-object of white desire, to infringe on the native acquisitiveness of whiteness.

The category "Latino," used as a racial descriptor rather than a political affiliation, is nearly as vague as "brown." Consider, for example, how easily "Latin" (or for that matter, "Spanish" and "Hispanic") may substitute for "Latino." However, most uses of "Latina/o" disregard the politics of that ambiguity, together with the differences that the category itself already collapses. Remarkably, queer theory understands the politics of difference as fundamental to its practice, yet it can participate in the circulation of categories like "Latin" without appreciating in the least its function within a complex web of identifications and desires. While the variations on the category "Latina/o" collapse innumerable differences, queer theorizing seems for the most part quite content to let that sameness alone. "Queer" needs to interrogate its own investments in sameness.

Ironically, these investments deploy the rhetoric of difference precisely so that the presumed anti-identity of queer might dissimulate profiting by sameness. By this means, establishmentarian queer theory has colluded in rendering material and psychic violences of racialization unintelligible.

I agree that communities are bound by fictions, but that does not diminish the violences enacted in constituting those communities. Queer theory has exchanged too hastily the politics of identity for the politics of difference. To combat oppression, it is necessary to theorize how communities are bound by shared fantasies and desires, in other words, how they are bound on some level by sameness. This is especially crucial where sameness makes itself transparent, as it does with whiteness. Sometimes, people are not so different from one another. Queer theory, when it privileges difference over sameness absolutely, colludes with institutionalized racism in vanishing, hence retrenching, white privilege. It serves as the magician's assistant to whiteness's disappearing act.

Hanson acknowledged that he had anticipated my response and had heard exactly the same protest before. Oddly, these repeated protests only invalidate one another. I should in fact feel shamed at this revelation of the commonplace nature of my thinking. Hanson's accusation constitutes a defensive posture, a way to dismiss criticism. However, I think the solace I received (much of it from white lesbian theorists) may similarly indicate a form of defensiveness. I absolutely experienced solidarity with white lesbian theorists at the conference, but there was also from some an expression of solace that I think masqueraded (and only just barely) as solidarity.[22] I am sure that reactions to the dispute between Hanson and me had to have been more complicated than the (apparent) polarization, the taking of sides that occurred after the final roundtable. But I also wonder if that (apparent) polarization did not in fact need to happen to preserve the status quo, to further bind queer theory's white indivisibility. As I alternately inhabited the body of an intransigent and vulgar savage as well as that of a noble one (depending on where you sat), as I performed my brownness—and what choice did I have, really, fated as I was to my performance of the unsophisticated and banal—I understood the rupture I witnessed as one that needed to happen in order to fortify that white body of queer theory, to strengthen its immunity against foreign agents. I did experience genuine intellectual engagement with colleagues. Otherwise, I would not waste my energy formulating this critique. However, that engagement was subsumed by a reductive polarization; like the brown body (poor Mario's, Kiko's, my own, and, most important, the brown body missing in action), it was an obligatory sacrifice to the status quo of Gay Shame's queer theorizing.

Although the ironies of Ellis Hanson's presentation were lost on me, I was keenly aware of another, much crueler irony. The brown body in his schoolboy uniform, invited into the university classroom of a cosmopolitan gay male fantasy for a game of show and tell, remains simultaneously shut out of the university classroom. Increasingly, the brown body finds itself expelled from civil society—if not expelled outright from the nation. Seeing Kiko up on the screen, his dick hanging out of his khaki shorts, made the absence of gay men and lesbians and trans people of color at the conference all that much more pronounced. The brown body is variously sacrificed at the exigencies of white privilege and white desire. As peculiar as this may sound, I am not convinced that institutionalized forms of queer theory really care to investigate desire. An established group of queer theorists remain quite riled, understandably, about the normalization of queer. However, queer theory resists the critique of its own even more alarming normalizations. The dominant queer culture, like any dominant culture, demands assimilation. Queer theory does not want to be normalized, but neither does it want to be queered. Unruly subjects are expelled to its margins. This expulsion is telling. Establishmentarian queer theory, despite its oft-professed revulsion at mass culture assimilation, has also quite comfortably settled at the center or, rather, that comfortably furnished space just left of center. We would be deluded to think that queer theory is not invested in protecting the institutional structures that have accommodated it, including, most significantly, white patriarchal structures of knowledge. This does not call for abandoning the field but rather for greater vigilance, imagination, and accountability, as well as a reinvigorated inquiry into the complex trajectories of desire and identity.

How Now, Brown Body? The Problematic of Enunciation

Under what conditions does eroticism mingle with political solidarity? When does it produce an effect of empowerment? When does identification imply objectification and when does it imply equality?
—Kobena Mercer, *Welcome to the Jungle: New Positions in Black Cultural Studies*

In 2009, David Halperin and Valerie Traub published a companion volume to the Gay Shame conference, including a revised version of Ellis Hanson's presentation, titled "Teaching Shame." Hanson ends the essay with a brief discussion of his turn to Kiko in his presentation on teaching Plato's *Symposium* and a response to his recollection of my critique from the conference. (Neither he nor Halperin and Traub reply to my published critique of the conference.) Hanson uses cultural critic Kobena Mercer to discipline me, concluding his chapter with a review of Mercer's two famous essays on Robert Mapplethorpe, published conjointly in *Welcome to the Jungle: New Positions in Black Cultural Studies* (1994) as "Reading Racial Fetishism: The Photographs of Robert Mapplethorpe." In particular, Hanson hopes to find in Mercer a fellow advocate for racial fetishism. In the process of recruiting Mercer to vindicate his own racial fetishism of Kiko, Hanson creates an analogy between himself and Mapplethorpe, between the images of Kiko and the photographs from *Black Book*. But his analogy is more opportunistic than substantive. I wonder if Hanson doesn't overstate his case in turning to Mercer for a defense of racial fetishism. After all, Mercer foregrounds his ambivalence in the first paragraph of his later reading of Mapplethorpe: "This revision arises not because those arguments [in the earlier essay] were wrong, but because I have changed my mind, or rather, I should say, I still cannot make up my mind about Mapplethorpe."[23] Nonetheless, Mercer indeed offers a much more generous reading of Mapplethorpe. He finds new contexts for reading the photographs. Mapplethorpe's death from AIDS, the attempts by Jesse Helms and other prominent conservative leaders to shut down federal arts funding, and the June 12, 1989, cancellation of a Mapplethorpe exhibition at the Corcoran Museum of Art provide new context for Mercer's reading: "this chain of events has irrevocably altered the context in which we perceive, evaluate and argue about the aesthetic and political value of Mapplethorpe's photographs" (Mercer 189).

Mercer's recovery of Mapplethorpe is based on what he identifies as the "mutuality" between the artist and his models. More than just photographer and passive objects, Mercer sees Mapplethorpe and his black models as members of a community. He locates mutuality in their shared social world:

Mapplethorpe's homoeroticism may be read as a highly stylized form of reportage which documented aspects of the urban gay cultural milieu of the post-Stonewall era of the 1970s. Historical changes in this urban gay cultural context, brought about partly as a result of AIDS in the 1980s, enable one to see what was art photography now as photographic documentary, recording a world that no longer exists in quite the same way it did before. (196)

More importantly, that mutuality provides ground for potential political alliances. Mercer locates in Mapplethorpe's photographs interracial identifications that are not only *not* necessarily exploitative but also potentially empowering. But Hanson is not Mapplethorpe, and his use of Kiko's body in "ironic" juxtaposition to his lecture on Plato does nothing to foster political solidarity. The brown body provides ornamentation for his presentation; Hanson forecloses mutuality rather than cultivating it.

Hanson insists on the irony of his performance, which includes donning the drag of Kiko's colonial schoolboy uniform. He invokes the ironic to isolate two audiences, those who get it and those who do not. The brown body provides the ground for ironizing but not the proper audience. Irony provides the alibi for Hanson's (and white gay male shame's) occupation of the brown body. Once again the brown body is reduced to spectacle vis-à-vis white gay male intellectual labor. Hanson's is the assassin's irony. As Mercer explains, "It is the problematic of enunciation that circumscribes the marginalized positions of subjects historically misrepresented or underrepresented in the dominant culture, for to be marginalized is to have no place from which to speak" (194).

Hanson's argument seems to be that everyone festishizes, so what's wrong with racial fetishism? "Is there someone who is never a sexual and racial fetishist? Is it somehow worse than being a gender fetishist (which is to say, a homosexual or a heterosexual)? What better purpose than fetishism has sexual and racial difference ever served?" he asks at the conclusion of his essay (162). He makes similar arguments about racial fetishism in an essay on Gary Fisher, whose work was edited and published posthumously by Eve Sedgwick in the volume *Gary in Your Pocket: Stories and Notebooks of Gary Fisher*. In that essay, "The Future's Eve: Reparative Reading after Sedgwick," he asks, "is there race without fetishism? Is there sex without fetishism?" (110). In addition to universalizing fetishism, he cites Tim Dean's argument that fetishism can be "impersonalizing" rather than dehumanizing. José Muñoz critiques Dean and Hanson on this point:

> But, of course, impersonalization as a process does not then preclude different individuals or groups from a very real sense of dehumanization in relation to systemic cultural and political logics like racism. Certain shared or collaborative projects of impersonalization are not automatically wounding and are often sexually generative, but these scenarios, for the most part, include a shared and volitional script.[24]

The mutuality Mercer speaks of in his recovery of Mapplethorpe suggests such a script, despite what appears to be the exploitative nature of *Black Book*. Such mutuality was absent from Hanson's enactment of racial fetishism at the conference.

Despite how Hanson positions me, I am not antipleasure or even antiporn. I am not anti–racial fetishism, though I find most expressions of it as dull as Hanson probably finds what he designates "Lesbian Piety." What I do object to is Hanson's refusal to consider how the psychic and social meet in racial fetishism and his isolation of the phenomenon from any operations of power. Muñoz takes Hanson to task:

> But the example of Fisher in Hanson's article does not telescope out to consider the world outside the page, it fails to consider the damage that racial fetishism does within the social or the ways in which racial fetishism can easily be a byproduct of racial oppression. To the contrary, his reading of the text attempts to hold this knowledge at bay. ("Race, Sex," 111)

Eroticism and political solidarity do not mingle in Hanson's treatment—and public enactment—of racial fetishism. Muñoz continues, "racial difference can be and often is erotic. But these fetishistic erotics don't exist in a vacuum or unmoor themselves from the fact of systemic racism. In white male culture the erotic value bestowed on men of color is often linked to devaluing them in other aspects of their being" ("Race, Sex," 111).

In some sense, I agree with Halperin and Traub's condescending account of what transpired during the closing panel of the conference: "What followed did not take a very pedagogical form. And it was as predictable as it was unsettling. Unwilling to resist the pull of a role that has all too often been constructed for people of color, Hiram Pérez dedicated his time on the final panel to detailing the racist offense of Hanson's presentation."[25] It did feel like I was fulfilling a role. And it felt inescapable. As Judith Halberstam describes, "Pérez found himself very much in the position of Montez: he could speak, but he would always be read as a queer of color performing as a person of color and leaving the space of articulation open to the real gay subjects: white gay men."[26] I do, however, contest Halperin and Traub's claim that "[w]hat followed did not take a very pedagogical form" (30). Their remarks in the introduction to the *Gay Shame* volume only serve to resume their disengagement with a race critique of the conference. They refuse also to consider how the role they claim I was "unwilling to resist" is one they reserved for me by limiting brown folks at the conference to only such embodied performances as might enable (or at least not obstruct) the work of white gay male shame. Although Halperin and Traub claim to have invited me to contribute to the *Gay Shame* volume, they do not mention that they specifically asked that my contribution not be the critique I delivered at the conference. In effect, they fashioned with their invitation a kind of containment by inclusion. As publishing something other than my critique would feel dishonest, I declined and ultimately published my essay with *Social Text*. The editors sought to fix the terms by which noncanonical bodies are allowed to access queer theory. The brown body, forbidden enunciation, remains a kind of communal property for a dominant cosmopolitan gay imagination, the object of its reactionary nostalgia. In the years since Gay Shame, queer of color critique, among other interventions, has productively challenged establishmentarian queer theory's intransigence to thinking race. Interestingly, one manner of response from the establishmentarian queer has been to declare the end of queer theory, in effect to close ranks.

5

Gay Cowboys Close to Home

Obviously not all gay, lesbian, and transgender people live their lives in radically different ways from their heterosexual counterparts, but part of what has made queerness compelling as a form of self-description in the past decade or so has to do with the way it has the potential to open up new life narratives and alternative relations to time and space.
—Judith Halberstam, *In a Queer Time and Place: Transgender Bodies, Subcultural Lives*

"You boys found a way to make the time pass up there, didn't you."
—Joe Aguirre to Jack Twist, "Brokeback Mountain"

During their first summer together on Brokeback Mountain, Ennis del Mar and Jack Twist famously proclaim that they are not queer. Ang Lee's film powerfully adapts this anxious exchange between the two protagonists of Annie Proulx's short story: "Ennis said, 'I'm not queer,' and Jack jumped in with 'Me neither. A one-shot thing. Nobody's business but ours.'"[1] Gay pundits too numerous to count and several major newspapers "jumped in" as well, eager to corroborate the nervous denunciations uttered by these two teenage protagonists. Representing an ideologically wide spectrum, writers weighed in on why Ennis and Jack—and the film itself—are not gay, much less queer. A headline from the gay and lesbian website *Advocate.com* decreed, "Not a gay movie."[2] Sometimes citing the movie's transcendence of identity categories, at other times impugning the political viability of identity categories altogether, critics across the country and internationally echoed the *Advocate*'s headline.[3]

It is remarkable that such overwhelming consensus about the meaning of gay and queer identities should greet the anxious repudiations of characters Proulx herself describes as "inarticulate, confused Wyoming ranch kids . . . [who] find themselves in a personal sexual situation they did not expect, understand, nor can manage."[4]

Questions about its political disposition (queer or mainstream) and the proper identity categories for its characters (straight, gay, or otherwise) loomed larger in the film's critical reception than its powerful affect, which for many viewers persists well beyond the devastating conclusion. (That affect in fact became grounds for dismissing the film as melodrama or a "chick flick.") This chapter offers a queer reading of *Brokeback Mountain*, focusing on the character Ennis del Mar, so often (mis)read as a repressed homosexual. Arguably, the "not a gay movie" response to *Brokeback Mountain* is symptomatic of unimaginative turns in gay and queer politics. Rather than opening new possibilities for identity, "not a gay movie" rules out any engagement with the inherent contradictions of identity, in effect foreclosing the alternative life narratives toward which *Brokeback Mountain* gestures.

The "not a gay movie" reading inadvertently naturalizes heterosexuality as well as quashing differences—contradictions even—that may inhabit "gay" or "queer." Furthermore, it risks making the violence in the film unnameable. The dispute over the film's queer identities calls for the revitalization of what Halberstam finds most compelling about queerness: "the way it has the potential to open up new life narratives and alternative relations to time and space."[5] In that spirit, this chapter contests the prevailing reading of Ennis del Mar as a repressed homosexual, instead inviting his difference to help open both "gay" and "queer" to new narratives. Ennis's queerness is concentrated unexpectedly in the cowboy ethic that guides his life; because nationally that ethic is memorialized as heroically and uniquely masculine, its queerness has dissipated from legend. This chapter restores the queer in cowboy, insisting that we situate Ennis close to home (Wyoming, ranch labor, rural) in order to fully appreciate his difference. Proulx offers that Jack and Ennis are "beguiled by the cowboy myth";[6] this chapter proposes that queerness is a quietly beguiling aspect of the myth.

David Leavitt's article for *Slate Magazine*—"Is Brokeback Mountain a Gay Film?"—exemplifies postmodern identity criticism generalized for a mass culture medium.[7] The article is nuanced, intelligent, and persuasive. It also advances, without necessarily naming it as such, an argument for reading the same-sex relationship in the film as an example of situational homosexuality. Leavitt's essay is framed with a concern about naming—its impossibility, its failures—that echoes the distrust of identity categories as adequate representations of individual experience. In the first paragraph, Leavitt writes that the "two dirt-poor cowboys find themselves suddenly caught up in a passion for each other that they have no idea how to name." The final paragraph praises the film's treatment of the inarticulacy of experience: "In the end, *Brokeback Mountain* is less the story of a love that dares not speak its name than of one that doesn't know how to speak its name, and is somehow more eloquent for its lack of vocabulary." It's difficult to disagree with Leavitt's assessment of the film, and both Lee and Proulx construct texts that are hauntingly eloquent in their representations of inarticulacy. My concern is for the propensity among critics to deem the love between Ennis and Jack unnameable and nonetheless name it "not gay." Leavitt, for instance, asks, "Is *Brokeback Mountain*, as it's been touted, Hollywood's first gay love story? The answer—in a very positive sense, I think—is yes to the love story, no to the gay." What exactly does Leavitt leave us at the other side of "not gay"? Does naming the identity with its negation really remove us from any of the identitarian tyranny that may follow the categorization "gay"? Much of Leavitt's reading of the film in fact invokes judgments that are consistent with gay liberation politics, raising doubt as to how far "not gay" removes us really from "gay." For example, Leavitt reads Ennis as the repressed partner in the relationship. ("What both men want, it becomes clear, is what Ennis is afraid to let them have.") The classification "not gay" apparently does not remove Ennis from the most canonical structure of the classification "gay": the closet.

Leavitt concludes, "The result is a defense of gay marriage made all the more eloquent by its evasion of the banalities implied in the word 'gay.'" He expresses a distaste for the identity category "gay," yet his reading suggests his investment in the gay liberalism of the day. Does *Brokeback Mountain* necessarily result in a defense of gay marriage? Such a reading, I argue, emerges from a particular investment not only in a gay metanarrative but also in the particular assimilationism defining contemporary gay and lesbian politics. The film might also be read as a critique against marriage, as I argue below. Leavitt is predisposed toward his interpretation of a "defense of gay marriage" the moment he determines that Ennis and Jack slip into "a kind of conjugal ease" as the action progresses. Such a reading invests in more traditional constructions of space and time. The model for the relationship is the conjugal one because there are no other models. While "gay" undergoes a species of deconstruction—albeit vulgar—the heterosexual institutions of conjugal space and time are naturalized. Leavitt argues, regarding Ennis's aversion to a more permanent (read "conjugal") model for the relationship, that "[i]t's as if he believes they don't deserve better." But doesn't this presume that the conjugal model is indeed the preferred construction for any romantic relationship? And does it presume that the "not gay" Ennis suffers from the very "gay" ailments of gay self-loathing and closetedness? My problem with the "not a gay movie" reading is not just that it tends to inadvertently naturalize heterosexuality but also that it quashes differences—contradictions even—that may inhabit "gay" or "queer."

Don't Fence Me In . . . or Out

In addition to critiques that either impugn or claim to transcend identity, yet another argument appeals to a gay authenticity presumably violated by *Brokeback Mountain*. Novelist Adam Mars-Jones, writing for the British paper the *Observer*, lambastes the film for its lack of a gay consciousness and complains that the project foregoes an authenticity he deems realizable only through the "actual testimony" of gay men.[8]

Curiously, despite the nature of his protest, Mars-Jones himself overlooks "actual testimony." Such disregard is typical of the entire body of "not a gay movie" criticism. Poised as self-appointed arbiters of what is gay or queer, these critics uniformly fail to consult potential archives for testimony from men situated similarly to the characters in the short story and film. Apparently it is not necessary to leave New York or San Francisco or London to write about Wyoming's "ranch-country" queer populations. Such testimonials, gathered by only a handful of reporters, disturb the identity fence posts staked by either gay liberalism or postmodernist queer theories. Much of the interpretation of Ennis's identity reads his silence as a relic of a bygone era when gay men were less likely to publicize their sexuality. This criticism ignores the significance of contemporary identifications with Ennis del Mar. Are the identifications articulated by Wyoming ranchers then also relics, or might they document instead counternarratives of gay identity? Where else might the trajectories of these identifications lead us?

Guy Trebay's *New York Times* report from Lusk, Wyoming, is one of the few newspaper or magazine accounts of reception of the film that bothers to seek the response of a gay rural audience. After a special screening in Jackson, Wyoming, Trebay quotes a thirty-three-year-old rancher, Derrick Glover, who proclaims, "That could have been my life." Glover's roots in Wyoming are deep, his family having "worked the land around Lusk for generations."[9] His identifications complicate the way we assess the choices Ennis makes. While critics repeatedly cite Ennis's repression, even judging him a "coward,"[10] Glover's testimony suggests alternative narratives. Defying the dominant narrative of queer desire to migrate from rural to urban, Glover explains, "I never had any intention of leaving the cowboy lifestyle. . . . Ranching is who I am." Criticism of the film, even when proclaiming the protagonists "not gay," privileges a narrowly defined terrain of sexuality as the primary locus of identity for queer subjects. For example, the nature of Ennis's relationships with Jack and Alma, as well as his one pronouncement against queer identification, functions to disqualify him from the classifications "gay" and "queer," but the criteria for sanctioning what counts as evidence need to be reevaluated. Our frame of reference for making determinations about sexual identity is too narrowly focused. Both humanist and posthumanist interrogations of sexuality may inadvertently collude with the hegemonic specification of individuals, as described by Foucault, through the truth of sex.[11] How are boundaries naturalized for the delimited field of activities, desires, and identifications that constitute sexuality? Might the narratives of *Brokeback Mountain*, including the testimonies it generates, broaden our frame of reference for determining sexual identities?

Glover's testimony defies categorization under the binary "in/out":

> "They always define it as coming out of the closet, but I don't consider myself to be out of the closet," Mr. Glover explained. There is a reason for that, he said. "Where I live, you can't really go out and be yourself. You couldn't go out together, two guys, as a couple and ever be accepted. It wasn't accepted in the past, it's still not, and I don't think it ever will be." That he and some of the others interviewed for this article were willing to be named and photographed was not without social and physical risk.[12]

Glover's experience resists the language of the closet. He distances himself from the dominant narrative for modern gay and lesbian identities, noting the canonization of the closet but attributing it to a hegemonic authority: "*They* always define *it*" (emphasis added). Glover presents a conundrum to the totalizing logic of the closet. He doesn't consider himself "out," yet, as Trebay points out, he remains "willing to be named and photographed" for a *New York Times* article on gay cowboys and the impact of *Brokeback Mountain*. The characterizations of Ennis in both the short story and film present comparable difficulties. Dominant narratives of gay identity fail to accommodate either Glover's testimony or Ennis del Mar's fiction.

Ben Clark, a "fourth generation rancher from Jackson," also identifying with the film's protagonists, testifies to the lack of an identity on which to model his own: "I grew up with the same kind of fear and conflict. . . . Growing up, I never even dreamed that a real cowboy would be gay."[13] As a part of his interview with Clark, Trebay shares a joke he's learned from his local sources: "There's a joke out here about how one goes about finding a gay man on the frontier. The punch line is deadpan: Look for the wife and kids." The joke suggests the frequency of the circumstance; the gay man is commonplace on the frontier. But furthermore, it asks that we reconsider a place for queer life vis-à-vis heterosexuality. The coming-out narrative fences in Ennis del Mar and fences him out as well. It canonizes the closet for queer life and imposes the binary "in/out" on Ennis del Mar regardless of whether or not that narrative construct translates meaningfully within the parameters of the story. A disputed interpretation of fiction is not all that is in question here. How we decide to read the fiction on this point may also impact how we greet sexual outsiders.

As Trebay's interviews reveal, the reactions to *Brokeback Mountain* unearth a potential archive. One part of that archive is comprised of the voices of Wyoming men testifying to their identifications with the film; another part is the cultural politics that the film ignites. But an archive only submits knowledge of other lives when it brings us into crisis, when we too arrive at a new understanding of ourselves and our desires. Halberstam's work on Brandon Teena, in which he shifts focus from the production of biography to an analysis of the stories told about him— what he designates as the "Brandon Archive"—offers a creative approach to the archive. The stories that *Brokeback Mountain* stirs to the surface, like the Brandon archive, reveal "how little we actually know about the forms taken by queer life outside of metropolitan areas."[14] Halberstam proposes that "Brandon's story, while cleaving to its own specificity, needs to remain an open narrative."[15] The remainder of this chapter reopens the narrative(s) in question through a series of provocations that nonetheless cleave to the specificities of the texts at hand.

Rather than acknowledge its content as potentially representative of a gay experience, the prevailing attitude seems to dictate that it is more radical to deny *Brokeback Mountain* status as a gay film because of its protagonists' resistance to naming themselves "gay" or "queer." John Wirt's review for the *Advocate* is typical in identifying repression as the singular motivation for Ennis's choices within the narrative. According to Wirt, "the repressed Ennis is the one who argues that a life together is impossible, that he and Jack must continue their traditional family-man existences in the conventional world, no matter how grim."[16] Wirt ignores the fact that Ennis, unlike Jack, has already abandoned a "family-man" existence. Is it possible that the unhappiness of his marriage makes him averse to pursuing a relationship similarly modeled, whether that be a heterosexual or a same-sex union? Might Ennis's refusal of a lifestyle modeled on the conventional heterosexual relationship in fact mark his queerness?

When a remarried and pregnant Alma tells Ennis that he should marry again, he responds sarcastically, "Once burned." Perhaps even more telling, standing in the kitchen helping Alma with the dishes after a family reunion over Thanksgiving dinner, Ennis "feel[s] too big for the room." He is not looking to settle down, being committed instead to a cowboy's transience, making his home in a trailer out of economic necessity but also because of lifestyle. Only Jack directly expresses dissatisfaction with the course of their relationship. Ennis communicates his longing for an absent Jack and a desire to prolong their encounters, but, in the short story at least, he never expresses dissatisfaction with the nature of the relationship. Like the fourth-generation rancher from Jackson, Ben Clark, interviewed by Trebay, Ennis finds himself at a loss, searching for some model that will help him comprehend his situation: "Shit. I been lookin at people on the street. This happen a other people? What the hell do they do?" (271). Ennis, then, hardly in denial or repressed, actively reflects on his difference and seeks (albeit unsuccessfully) an alternative expression of his identity.

In opposition to Jack's desire for domesticity modeled on marriage, Ennis's commitment in the relationship suggests an alternative (or queer) temporality. After all, the urgency and intensity of their desire is dictated by the fleetingness of their encounters. Readings of the film as a defense of gay marriage abound, yet there is no indication in either short story or film that Jack's and Ennis's passion can weather domestication. Ennis cherishes the ephemeral, a quintessentially queer measure of time and space. As if to confirm that he is as serious about his model for the relationship as Jack is about domesticity, he cites the magnitude of his sacrifices, reminding Jack that "[t]hem earlier days I used a quit the jobs" (277). The idyllic space and time of Brokeback Mountain, enshrined in memory and rekindled during passionate but fleeting encounters, sustains Ennis. The pain and frustration of repeated departure perhaps enflames Ennis's pleasure, while Jack's pain remains unambivalent. Jack confronts Ennis on this point:

> "Tell you what, we could a had a good life together, a fuckin real good life. You wouldn't do it, Ennis, so what we got now is Brokeback Mountain. Everything built on that. . . . You got no fuckin idea how bad it gets. I'm not you. I can't make it on a couple a high-altitude fucks once or twice a year." (277–78)

The prevailing reading of Ennis's resistance to Jack's proposition, perhaps due to the political imperatives of the current gay liberalism, interprets his refusal of the "good life together" to repression and self-loathing. Jack's accusations suggest an alternative reading. For Ennis, loss is tinged with pleasure.

The transitory nature of the relationship is a comfort as well as a burden. This quality is more pronounced in Proulx's short story, diminished in the film by additional dialogue. In both texts, Jack declares, "I wish I knew how to quit you." McMurtry and Ossana provide Ennis a response, with content and affect arguably extraneous to the short story. As he chokes back tears, Ennis answers Jack, "Then why don't you? Why don't you just let me be, huh? It's because of you Jack that I'm like this. I'm nothing; I'm nowhere." Ennis struggles to break free from Jack's embrace before collapsing into his arms. Through his tears, he complains, "I can't stand this anymore, Jack." This articulation of grief and regret on the part of Ennis is unique to the film. In the short story, his legs cave underneath him in response to Jack's tirade, but the substance of Ennis's affect remains more ambiguous. Rushing to him, Jack cannot "guess if it was heart attack or the overflow of an incendiary rage" that drops Ennis to his knees. Even transposing onto the original McMurtry's and Ossana's verbalization of Ennis's affect, the question of his disposition toward Jack's proposal remains open. Jack may well have made Ennis "like that"; nonetheless, he remains disinclined toward Jack's solution. It is that disinclination that I argue needs to be reopened, reassessed, complicated.

Reading the short story next to the film is useful on this point. For instance, in the story Ennis not only relishes the time stolen with Jack but also, after the death of his lover, the scent of Jack Twist's shirt, the occasional dream of Jack. This presents a major difference from the film's adaptation. The Ennis del Mar of the film remains too solemn to appreciate such ephemera. His attachment to Jack's old shirt is rendered mournful, some might argue maudlin. The Ennis del Mar of the short story is not a man devoid of pleasure and not as devastated as his cinematic counterpart. When Proulx introduces her reader to Ennis, he has just awoken before sunrise, preparing himself to be displaced by a real estate development that shuts down the ranch that employs him. The setting is stark, his future bleak:

> The wind booms down the curved length of the trailer and under its roaring passage he can hear the scratching of fine gravel and sand. It could be bad on the highway with the horse trailer. He has to be packed and away from the place that morning. . . . He might have to stay with his married daughter until he picks up another job. (255)

But then Proulx shows us another side to Ennis, a glance inside the man that the film does not offer. He is alone, facing unemployment and uncertainty, "yet he is suffused with a sense of pleasure because Jack Twist was in his dream" (255). Ennis may be haunted by ephemera, but he is also comforted. He discovers after Jack's death his lover's "old shirt from Brokeback days," Ennis's own shirt hidden inside, "the sleeves carefully worked down inside Jack's sleeves" (283). Jack's death has not robbed Ennis of a romantic imagination; the shirt inspires longing in him but also reignites his capacity for sensual pleasure: "He pressed his face into the fabric and breathed in slowly through his mouth and nose, hoping for the faintest smoke and mountain sage and salty sweet stink of Jack but there was no real scent, only the memory of it, the imagined power of Brokeback Mountain of which nothing was left but what he held in his hand" (283). The image is not entirely bleak; the regenerative power of memory and imagination prevail. In the scene that follows, Ennis orders a postcard of Brokeback Mountain that he will pin up in his trailer above the two shirts. The "ensemble" elicits from him "stinging tears," evoking a sentimentalist image of Ennis that conflicts with interpretations that read him as uniformly stoic and repressed.

The postcard memorializes precisely the transient nature of the relationship between the two men, one negotiated over long distances not by phone but by postcards used to arrange dates and locations of their rare meetings. Again, this testifies to how Ennis is gratified by ephemera. Jack's absence provides a source of both pain and pleasure for Ennis; his attitude to their separation suggests more ambivalence than critics have allowed. It is in part the childlike delight with which the film's Ennis receives each postcard that makes it so crushing when he emerges from the post office holding in his hand not a new card from Jack but rather his own missive returned, marked "DECEASED." It is essential also to recall, before assessing Ennis's position on his physical separation from Jack, how the experience on Brokeback Mountain idealized by both characters—but, as Jack charges, more so by Ennis—is one of desire repeatedly frustrated by distance, repeatedly rewarded with love. They never remain in camp together for longer than a night, as one must travel back and forth several hours a day to tend the sheep. If Ennis seeks to regain the fulfillment he experienced on Brokeback, it makes sense that he would pursue a script that calls for prolonged absences punctuated with abbreviated but intense reunions in favor of a script that realizes a more regularly dependable (i.e., domesticated) presence of the loved object. It is clear in both the short story and the film that only Jack insists on permanence.

Gay Cowboys in Close Range

In an interview for a Wyoming newspaper, Proulx objects to the categorization of the film as a "gay cowboy" movie. "Excuse me . . . but it is not a story about 'two cowboys.'"[17] Despite Proulx's objection, there is an argument to be made for considering Ennis a modern-day cowboy. If he's not yet a cowboy on Brokeback Mountain (where he works as a shepherd), he certainly becomes one in the remainder of the story. Jack, too, before settling into his bourgeois existence with Lureen, makes a living as a rodeo cowboy. In fact, Ennis's derision of the rodeo cowboy—more pronounced in the film—raises its own questions of authentic masculinity within both texts. If Ennis is the authentic cowboy, then we cannot expect him to settle down. Domesticity is anathema to a cowboy lifestyle, traditionally understood.

The invention of barbed wire, privatization of land, and modernization eventually restrict the original cowboy's habitat to Wild West shows. He disappears together with the open range; whether or not Jack and Ennis are cowboys is then also a matter of symbolism. The cowboy roams the popular imagination, well past his life driving cattle over large expanses of Texas and the American West. Apart from the specific historical register, the title of "cowboy" also marks a lifestyle, characteristically rugged and independent. Ennis's hard, itinerant work life arguably makes him a modern-day cowboy. I use "itinerant" specifically to characterize the instability of his career, while geographically he remains stationed in Wyoming, his lack of mobility a matter both of choice and of economics. Ennis tolerates the erratic lifestyle of ranch work in order to preserve his independence. As Proulx describes, "Ennis went back to ranch work, hired on here and there, not getting much ahead but glad enough to be around stock again, free to drop things, quit if he had to, and go into the mountains at short notice" (272). Ironically, the itinerancy of ranch work allows Ennis his independence but ultimately also severely limits his mobility. He is subject not only to the possibility of ranch foreclosure or sale but also to the fluxes of seasonal work (the amount of work available to Ennis, for example, depends at times on whether or not cows are calving and how many). These conditions apply when we first meet him in the film (Aguirre hires Jack and Ennis as seasonal laborers), and they are true in the short story when Proulx introduces the reader to Ennis as he prepares once more to relocate and find new work. In McMurtry's and Ossana's screenplay, Alma proposes that Ennis apply for work at a power plant, a job with long-term security and benefits. Ennis balks at the idea. Likewise, in the short story, Alma resents "his failure to look for a decent permanent job with the county or the power company" (272).

Proulx in fact describes Ennis's inclination toward ranch work as a "yearning" (271). He is like the rancher Derrick Glover, who affirms his devotion to the "cowboy lifestyle," insisting that *New York Times* readers regard his identity on terms he sets: "Ranching is who I am." His use of the word "lifestyle" resonates in this context due to its familiar usage in designating modern homosexuality the "gay lifestyle." Might not all cowboys be just a little gay? In his more expansive understanding of queerness, Halberstam includes "people who live without financial safety nets, without homes, without steady jobs, outside the organizations of time and space that have been established for the purposes of protecting the rich few from everyone else" among those people who "could productively be called 'queer subjects.'"[18] If we enlarge the word "queer" in the way that Halberstam suggests, the "cowboy lifestyle" indeed appears fundamentally queer. Readings that deny Ennis his queerness err by not accounting for his cowboy ethic. His values as a cowboy may prove elemental to his particular expression of queerness. Regarding the cowboy and his social status, historian Richard W. Slatta explains, "Cowboys held distinctive cultural values. These values and their way of life set them apart from others in society. In some cases, they occupied a unique legal status—that of rural outlaws or vagrants. By definition, they never owned land, exercised political power, or held high social position."[19] The designation "outlaw" need not imply criminality; the cowboy ethic of "use rights" suggests a radically different relationship to land, resources, and community in contrast to privatization. This ethic, however, clearly situates the cowboy outside the law. This same ethic is intrinsic to Ennis's queerness.

A historical examination of his career invites further queering. The American "cowboy" finds his forebear in the Spanish *vaquero*, or "cow-man."[20] The translation from "man" to "boy" situates the cowboy out of proper reproductive time. He represents a kind of instability, marked certainly by the constant movement of his calling. The exclusively male world of the cowboy lifestyle also removes him from reproductive time. As a pejorative, "boy" also marks class and race differences. The *vaquero* originates in Mexico, a mestizo figure employed by white Creoles; his U.S. successor, the cowboy, was often black. These class and race differences are sexualized and arguably also queer the body of the cowboy. It is striking really that "gay cowboy" should pose such a conceptual difficulty, at least for U.S. audiences.

While there is plenty to qualify the cowboy as a queer subject, he is also an iconic point of reference for American identity: masculine, heroic, independent. A tension arises between the cowboy's historical queerness and his role as national symbol. His queer reputation is a secret entrusted to the national imaginary. Chris Packard argues persuasively for the cowboy's forgotten queer life in his study *Queer Cowboys: And Other Erotic Male Friendships in Nineteenth-Century American Literature* (2005):

Particularly in Westerns produced before 1900, references to lusty passions appear regularly, when the cowboy is on the trail with his partners, if one knows how to look for them. In fact, in the often all-male world of the literary West, homoerotic affection holds a favored position. A cowboy's partner, after all, is his one emotional attachment, aside from his horse, and he will die to preserve that attachment. Affection for women destroys cowboy *comunitas* and produces children, and both are unwanted hindrances to those who wish to ride the range freely.[21]

Queer passions, as Packard points out, are not necessarily self-evident. They become apparent *if* "one knows how to look for them." And if an entire era of renegade queerness can disappear from the sanctioned memory of the nation, is it so unusual really that the queerness of a single, fictional cowboy should evaporate with so little critical pressure? Knowing how to look requires also knowing where to look, and neither the dominant culture nor the larger body of queer scholarship is attuned to the potential queerness of spaces outside the metropole and temporalities not measured by "coming out." The terrain of what constitutes sexuality also needs to be destabilized if we are to pursue satisfactorily the question of what identities Ennis represents.

We need to reckon, for instance, with Ennis's "yearning for low-paid, long-houred ranch work" (271–72). Some yearning clearly is satisfied by his ranch work, and some part of that satisfaction is sensual. The short story suggests a sensual gratification in the smells and sounds of ranch work, oddly, in its description of the conjugal bedroom after the birth of Alma Jr.: "their bedroom was full of the smell of old blood and milk and baby shit, and the sounds were of squalling and sucking and Alma's sleepy groans, all reassuring of fecundity and life's continuance to one who worked with livestock" (264). The passage both suggests Ennis's heterosexuality (he is comforted by his inclusion in that fecundity) and simultaneously undercuts any such reading, comparing the sounds and smells of his bedroom to that of livestock. But what should be emphasized here is his sensual pleasure, which need not be classified within the binary heterosexual/homosexual. Might not the sensuality of his work complicate the way we assess Ennis's sexuality? How is his sexuality potentially channeled through his work as a wrangler and ranch hand?

Why assume that his yearning for a cowboy lifestyle is not continuate with sexual desire? Jack hypothesizes an association between wrangling and sex when after intercourse he observes, "Christ, it got a be all that time a yours a horseback makes it so goddamn good" (267). Is it impossible that Ennis's labor on the ranch provides sensual—even sexual—gratification? Does the Proulx text suggest we include Ennis's cowboy lifestyle within his narrative sexuality? How does this square with the text's so-called "gay bona fides"?[22] If we allow for the sensuality of Ennis's work, we also need to consider the context of masculine camaraderie in which it transpires and the correlation then of sensual pleasure with male companionship.

Ennis's "cowboy lifestyle" in this modern context—which incorporates but cannot be reduced to queer sexuality—is arguably the greater threat to heteronormativity and the American way of life: migrant, exclusively homosocial, communal, anti-industrial. As documented in Proulx's collection *Close Range: Wyoming Stories* (which includes "Brokeback Mountain"), the days of a western frontier are long gone. The cowboys disappear together with the open ranges (leaving us Proulx's "Close Range"). However, what remains unequivocally, if now anxiously, is the cowboy as style. That style is less certain of its masculinity after *Brokeback Mountain*, a consolation for those of us weary of hearing the words "gay cowboy" serve as their own punch line. Both film and short story rupture the iconic masculinity of the cowboy and thus destabilize what is perhaps the emblematic masculinity of American individualism and courage. Where have all the cowboys gone, indeed. They've gone fishing.

As the title *Close Range* provocatively implies, all of the stories are about place, violence, and intimacy. The violence usually is consummated; the intimacy remains frustrated. The title evokes both home on the range and the sight on a shotgun. As indicated, all the stories are set in Wyoming. In this sense, Ennis is of Wyoming, and the scope of Proulx's work will not release him from that place. Throughout Proulx's work, place figures prominently in the lives of her characters. She asserts in an interview, "Everything that happens to characters comes welling out of place. Even their definition of themselves."[23] The film, too, with its languorous treatment of the mountainous landscape, performs a seduction, aligning the spectator's identifications with Ennis's and Jack's sensual—ultimately erotic—attachment to place. Ennis is indeed stuck in Wyoming, since mobility is not feasible, but is it not possible as well that other ties bind him to this place, ties that an urban queer bias especially may eclipse? Rather than merely stuck, he is perhaps rooted in the Wyoming landscape, its life and communities. The urban bias typical of gay and lesbian dominant cultures precludes recognition of the complex of identifications that may root someone like Ennis del Mar to a small-town or rural setting. Recall Derrick Glover's testimony: "I never had any intention of leaving the cowboy lifestyle. . . . *Ranching is who I am*" (emphasis added). As Halberstam observes, "Some queers need to leave home in order to become queer, and others need to stay close to home in order to preserve their difference."[24]

Comparisons of Ennis and Jack often ignore their differing socioeconomic statuses. Ennis is quick to point out these difference when Jack insists on meeting more regularly. Critics point to Ennis's resistance to relocating with Jack as evidence of his repressed identity, but they ignore that Ennis must forego meeting Jack, constrained by his economic circumstances. Repression does not explain Ennis's refusal to meet more regularly with Jack; the story indicates his desire to do so. The evidence in the story more strongly supports economic hardship and ties to place (including his relationship to his daughters) as Ennis's rationale for resisting Jack's demands for more than "a couple of high-altitude fucks once or twice a year." Ennis protests Jack's insensitivity to his economic situation: "Jack, I got a work. Them earlier days I used a quit the jobs. You got a wife with money, a good job. You forget how it is bein broke all the time" (277). Economics and place also circumscribe what identities are available to each character, a condition also ignored by the film's critics. Jack's rise in social class through his marriage to Lureen enables his greater mobility. That mobility makes it possible for Jack to adopt an identity closer to what contemporary spectators, especially urban gay men, recognize as modern and gay.

The metanarrative for that modern gay identity is largely founded on migration—to metropolitan locales, such as New York and San Francisco—and on a certain gay cosmopolitanism. Jack's sex tourism in Mexico is inferred in the short story and literalized in the film. Following a frustrated attempt to join Ennis after learning of his divorce, Jack goes to Mexico, where he cruises for sex. His greater mobility, especially his ability to travel outside the boundaries of the nation, contributes to an articulation of sexuality that many viewers more readily label as "gay" in comparison to the narrative they confront in Ennis. That story complicates the metanarrative for modern gay identity by insisting on an unfamiliar context. The experience of a poor, white, rural ranch hand, settled far from any metropolis, disrupts the usual narrative. Jack's trip to Mexico similarly defamiliarizes the cowboy, in this case by reintroducing him to queer origins. Although much criticism is devoted to the authenticity of the movie and its characters (i.e., are they gay? are they really cowboys? what is masculinity?), there is no commentary on the story's own play on authenticity. Jack, a belt-buckle cowboy of sorts, finds his rodeo-ing disparaged as inauthentic by Ennis, who claims "the kind of riding that interested him lasted longer than eight seconds and had some point to it" (260). In his travels, Jack retraces the migration of the original cowboys, the *vaqueros*, from the American West to Mexico. If such migration was crucial to the identity of the cowboy, it proves equally crucial to a modern gay sensibility, as the conflicting characterizations of Jack and Ennis establish. Jack proposes to Ennis, "We ought to go south. We ought a go to Mexico one day." He disregards the economic restrictions on Ennis's mobility; as Ennis explains, "Mexico? Jack, you know me. All the travelin I ever done is goin around the coffeepot lookin for the handle." Jack's migrations—his class mobility, his actual mobility, his cosmopolitanism in the form of sex tourism in Mexico—constitute the modern gay identity, or a nascent form of it, that so many critics appreciate in him. He even identifies the classic gay migration, from rural and small-town to urban, when—responding to Ennis's question about whether their situation is a common one—he proposes, "It don't happen in Wyomin and if it does I don't know what they do, maybe go to Denver." Demonstrating exactly the bias that renders Jack gay and/or brave and Ennis cowardly, repressed, and/or "not gay," Leavitt cites this passage to establish Jack's gay sensibility, claiming Denver as "possible urban refuge."[25] He does not ask whether the urban can ever really provide refuge to someone like Ennis. Might Ennis be that kind of queer who needs "to stay close to home in order to preserve [his] difference"? Or does such yearning render him inauthentic?

What we discover in fact—further complicating the question of Jack's authenticity—is that the cowboy is predecessor to the gay cosmopolitan. The travels of both cowboy and cosmopolitan serve colonial interests in expansion and westernization. The nation tolerates the cowboy's queerness in the nineteenth century as part of an unspoken compact. As Packard explains, "The cowboy is queer because audiences want him to be queer. America's official emblem of masculinity is not one who settles down after he conquests . . . [H]e moves on, perpetually conquering, and repeatedly affirming his ties to the wilderness and his male partner."[26] The Anglo cowboy's homosexuality is critical to westward expansion. His sexuality is quietly sanctioned by the nation, as is the racial violence he executes against American Indians, as well as Mexican ranchers who remained in Texas, and even Basque sheepherders. That violence will not be delayed by the demands of family life, and the cowboy fulfills his role in the colonization of the American West.

If the cowboy is recuperated as hero after his demise due to land privatization, this recuperation is perhaps due to a need to recast his role (and consequently that of the nation) in the violent settlement of the American West. The wilderness of the Wild West was characterized by the absence of U.S. legal jurisdiction. The Anglo cowboy's theft of Mexican cattle satisfied U.S. colonial interests. His outlaw behavior, in terms both of his theft and his queer sexuality, proved fortuitous for U.S. imperialism. However, it would need to be recast after the formal annexation of the West in order to preserve the nation's heroic fictions. "Cow-Boy," according to James Wagner, was originally applied to cattle thieves as early as the Revolutionary War, when it also functioned as a derogatory name for British Loyalists or traitors.[27] This more ambiguous legend of cowboy as traitor, foreigner, thief, and homosexual is nonetheless memorialized in the persistence of the word "cowboy," for despite its etymology, it survives with greater currency than less historically conflicted titles, such as "stockman," "cowhand," or "cowpuncher." In a remarkable example of the cowboy's conflicted historical reputation, Wagner quotes army officer Lt. S. H. Lincoln, writing from Fort Concho on September 16, 1875: "My camp was attacked last night by Indians or Cow-Boys."[28] Typically opposed in the construction "cowboys and Indians," here the two become exchangeable in their role as outlaws. If "cowboy" was once pejorative, as its omission from nineteenth-century dictionaries supports,[29] it becomes a romantic, heroic designation by the early twentieth century. His turbulent career, including those queer days on the open prairie, becomes a national secret, encapsulated in the preservation of the "boy" in his title. Perhaps "gay cowboy" suggests a redundancy rather than a punch line.

His original charge of racist violence completed, the cowboy, in his contemporary manifestation, finds himself the object of eradication. *Close Range* chronicles the struggle of Wyoming's poor whites toiling to reconcile frontier ethics with the impositions of modern life. In Ennis's case, his Spanish surname suggests that he is perhaps heir to the misfortune of those Mexican ranchers, Amerindians, or Basque and Hispanic sheepherders once subject to the Anglo cowboy's violence. Ennis del Mar, cowboy, is casualty to late capitalism. That surname—Spanish for "of the sea"—suggests ironically a cowboy out of his element. It also summons a cosmopolitan mobility that is the opposite of Ennis's landlocked situation.

Ennis and Jack on the Q.T.

It is precisely Ennis's refusal to accommodate Jack's demands for domesticity that may disturb some gay assimilationists. In this time of gay and lesbian assimilation, such a rejection is read as reactionary when it might also be read as queer. The story's Brokeback Mountain is all about queer time and space. It is the site where two "high school dropout country boys with no prospects" (256) etch out a time "when they owned the world and nothing seemed wrong" (255). Ultimately, Jack Twist embraces a bourgeois lifestyle (this is especially true in the film's expanded vision of Jack's life in Childress). His plans for Ennis and himself, for example, remain contingent on patriarchal logic in the form of the anticipated inheritance of property from his father and the potential payoff from Lureen's father, disdainful of his daughter's interclass marriage. Hence, the future he imagines with Ennis does not so much reflect the subversion of traditional constructions of space and time that characterized the season on Brokeback Mountain. Jack aspires rather to a more conventional temporality premised on the inheritance of his father's ranch and his assumption of domesticity together with Ennis instead of Lureen. Ennis, on the other hand, organizes time against the demands of normative temporality—he ultimately succumbs to those demands but stakes his oppositionality nonetheless, acquiescing for example to Jack's demands that he take additional days off work and extend his leaves from Alma and family duty. That oppositionality is also staked by his "cowboy lifestyle"—his refusing, for example, the power plant job.

It's possible that the domesticity that Jack projects as the appropriate shared desire might also represent in the story the end of Ennis's relationship to Jack as he knows and cherishes it. Ennis's time with Jack is time stolen from the demands of family and labor. Jack's time with Ennis is a lien on future time premised on a more conventional way of being. On Brokeback Mountain, Ennis and Jack share the same conceptions of time; they resist the demands of capital accumulation, defying

Joe Aguirre's instructions to maintain separate camps in order to secure the highest return on his flock. Aguirre's only interest is in preserving a privately owned flock of sheep on public land. Unknown to Ennis and Jack, Aguirre spies on them with binoculars. Having purchased their labor, Aguirre considers that the two have foregone privacy; their labor and hence their bodies become leased property. When Jack returns the following year once again seeking seasonal labor on Brokeback Mountain, and clearly hopeful to reunite with Ennis, he is confronted by a contemptuous Aguirre. Jack's inquiry for work is met with the foreman's sarcasm: "You boys found a way to make the time pass up there, didn't you" (269). It is not a question. Aguirre's retort is meant as an accusation. Although Jack does not report the remainder of the encounter to Ennis, the foreman has made it clear that he understood fully how "the boys" passed their time: "Twist, you guys wasn't getting paid to leave the dogs baby-sit the sheep while you stemmed the rose" (269).

The prevailing gay liberal reading of the story eulogizes the relationship as the unrealized marriage between Ennis and Jack. But Ennis does not lose Jack to societal prohibitions against gay marriage; he loses Jack to a gay bashing, a fact that makes the "not a gay movie" reading somewhat baffling. In the short story, Ennis's memories of the relationship are not morbid, and there is no indication of regret. There are alternative ways to recall the relationship, alternative narratives that also recast the story's significance to cultural politics. Aguirre's condemnation serves to remind us that Jack and Ennis are also two queers cruising each other in a public park. As such, they subvert state and dominant-culture prohibitions against not only same-sex desire but also public sex. "They never talked about sex, let it happen, at first only in the tent at night, then in the full daylight with the hot sun striking down, and at evening in the fire glow, quick, rough, laughing and snorting, no lack of noises" (262). These boys can hardly represent the decent, upstanding citizens of gay assimilationism.

Aguirre's classification of Ennis and Jack as "boys" places them outside of reproductive time (raising the specter of that queer cowboy).

The foreman's accusation about how they "pass the time" impugns Ennis and Jack for mingling work time with private time (they are just passing time, as opposed to working) and for their proscribed homosexual activity, conducted during working hours and in a public campsite. Ennis and Jack subvert the logic of time and space formally allocated for either private labor or public recreation. It is the queer time and space of Brokeback Mountain, repeatedly invoked, that lends its name both to Proulx's and Lee's texts. If we focus on the time and space of the mountain and the value subsequently attributed to it throughout the story, the case for queer readings of both texts hardly seems controversial. In order to dispute *Brokeback Mountain*'s status as gay or queer, critics focus instead on an unrealized (and definitively more conventional) future projected onto the story. The queer time and space of Brokeback Mountain subverts the respectable gay morality of contemporary assimilationist politics. We should not be surprised then that the film's queer content has been suppressed by a gay liberalism so intensely devoted to establishing gay and lesbian respectability to the exclusion of any other queer articulations of experience and identity. When first assigning his workers their charge, Aguirre explains that one of them will have to sleep with the sheep. One of the men will have to camp illegally, outside of the Forest Service–designated campsite. Pointing to Jack, Aguirre instructs, "pitch a pup tent on the q.t." (257). What their foreman does not anticipate is that the "boys" will translate "q.t." as queer time. Aguirre requires that Jack and Ennis violate Forest Service regulations on the quiet. Sanctioning this one transgression of the state regulation of public lands, Aguirre inadvertently sets in motion subsequent transgressions. Brokeback Mountain represents a rupture of the normative strictures of masculinity, labor, and publicity. What emerges on the horizon of that rupture is a queer time and space.

It must be noted that the relationship on Brokeback Mountain duplicates the gendered roles of traditionally conceived marriage, the husband performing the labor outside the home/camp, while the wife cooks, tends home/camp, and faithfully awaits his return. Jack at one point arrives at an empty campsite (no dinner, no wife), and when Ennis—delayed by his encounter with a bear—returns, Jack stereotypically explodes. Clearly, Jack and Ennis disagree over their futures, but perhaps also their recollections of Brokeback Mountain are not as harmonious as may superficially appear. The tension in the story may be defined in the following way: Jack Twist commemorates Brokeback Mountain as a rehearsal for marriage; Ennis del Mar commemorates Brokeback Mountain as a queer time and space, an evasion and deferral of the law in classic cowboy style. Jack privileges the permanence rehearsed on the mountain, Ennis its transcendent moments.

However, Jack's own reverie, following his emotional confrontation with Ennis during their last meeting, both fuels and defies his fetish for permanence. "What Jack remembered and craved in a way he could neither help nor understand was the time that distant summer on Brokeback when Ennis had come up behind him and pulled him close, the silent embrace satisfying some shared and sexless hunger" (278). In the film, the reverie takes the form of a flashback abruptly following the confrontation. The flashback disorients the viewer, incongruous both with the volatility of the previous scene and with the nature of Jack's demands. It is a moment marked by its singularity: "that dozy embrace solidified in his memory as the single moment of artless, charmed happiness in their separate and difficult lives" (279). However much he craves it, the moment cannot be reiterated:

> They had stood that way for a long time in front of the fire, its burning tossing ruddy chunks of light, the shadow of their bodies a single column against the rock. The minutes ticked by from the round watch in Ennis's pocket, from the sticks in the fire settling into coals. Stars bit through the wavy heat layers above the fire. Ennis's breath came slow and quiet, he hummed, rocked a little in the sparklight and Jack leaned against the steady heartbeat, the vibrations of the humming like faint electricity and, standing, he fell into sleep that was not sleep but something else drowsy and tranced. (278–79)

The watch is Aguirre's, given to Ennis to ensure that he promptly meet the supply truck on Fridays at noon. A marker of normative time, it is absorbed into the transcendence of the moment, reclaimed by the queer temporality of the embrace, measured in burning sticks, heartbeats, humming, gentle rocking, and slow breaths. Jack and Ennis's q.t. engulfs the normative function of the watch. The interruption of the action with this flashback produces a momentary incoherence in the film. Jack's most profound longing refuses to cohere with the normative temporality for which he pines.

In this sense, Ennis seems to intuit something about his desire that Jack cannot. Ennis longs not only for Jack's companionship but also for the conditions of Brokeback Mountain. Their encounters, eventually to Jack's protest, replicate those conditions. Ennis wants to remain outside—in every way. His particular attachment to Brokeback Mountain represents a way of life (consistent with a cowboy ethic) occluded in the prevailing readings of the film by the preeminence of another lifestyle narrative, the gay lifestyle as it is being narrowly defined by a dominant gay and lesbian constituency. If we regard Ennis as gay, then we also reopen the narrative for what "gay lifestyle" and "gay" can mean. Classifying Ennis as gay does not necessarily mean uncritically imposing on him an identity metanarrative; it can also constitute an invitation for men like Ennis to expand our understandings of "gay" and "queer" identities. Certainly, if we are not attentive to the constitutive power of identity politics, we risk the foreclosure of alterity, but "not gay" forecloses without the engagement that makes new, alternative narratives for identity intelligible. Ennis's difference remains "close to home" and far from the dominant narrative for gay identity. Movements that bear the names "gay" or "queer" are obligated to represent outsider sexualities; they should in fact welcome the contradictions an Ennis del Mar introduces to the under-interrogated truth of sex. The representations in Brokeback Mountain prevail on that "truth" to remain productively incomplete; they urge us to approach identity politics not with hostility but with imagination. Ennis, "too big for the room," ruptures the claustrophobic strictures of the "not a gay movie" debate. As gay cowboy he reopens a range for identity long-rived by the barbed wire and property claims of closed narratives for sexual intelligibility.

Space Cowboys

David Leavitt was not alone among critics in locating *Brokeback Mountain*'s cinematic eloquence in its study of inarticulacy. Critics read that inarticulacy, especially regarding the life of feelings, as archetypically masculine, embodied in the figure of Ennis. The theme of inarticulacy runs throughout the work of Annie Proulx, although not restricted to her male characters. *Close Range* has its share of female characters caged by language. However, that inarticulacy may represent more than a preferred character flaw for Proulx; it may also indicate the author's attention to the failings of language and human communication. The question that remains with me after reviewing criticism on the film does not concern Ennis's inarticulacy so much as a potentially diminished capacity to listen to him. On the one hand, language will not serve Ennis to communicate his experience of the world. We might account for this failure of the word by what Leo Bersani characterizes as the "dysfunctional relation of our language to our bodies."[30] On the other hand, that dysfunction arguably also encumbers Ennis's listeners. Rather than pathologize his inarticulacy, we might reconsider our own capacity to listen imaginatively when confronted with unfamiliar paradigms for identity.

It is useful in this regard to recall the imperative that Barbara Johnson establishes for the practice of reading, that "one set oneself up to be surprised by otherness." As Johnson explains,

> What the surprise encounter with otherness should do is lay bare some hint of an ignorance one never knew one had. . . . If I perceive my ignorance as a gap in knowledge instead of an imperative that changes the very nature of what I think I know, then I do not truly experience my

ignorance. The surprise of otherness is that moment when a new form of ignorance is suddenly activated as an imperative.[31]

If LGBT politics mean to redistribute power, then they need to check their own identity fences. What identities are fenced outside the boundaries of what we often too easily claim as community? A queer movement should struggle to recognize subjectivities that its own language might render unrepresentable. Regardless of whether or not subjects adopt the moniker "queer" or "gay," the movements that bear those names still need to responsibly represent outsider sexualities. "Responsibly" in this instance may also mean "imaginatively." In other words, the representations remain productively incomplete; they remain open narratives.

Years ago, I heard the poet Nikki Giovanni declare that if scientists really wanted to learn if there is life in outer space, they would send black women to find out. I wish to idealize Giovanni's claim about black women for a queer hermeneutic. The queer astronaut who invites the "surprise of otherness" would become adept at discerning unfamiliar forms of life. I would like to believe that. However, such life forms may well walk among us, for better or worse, undetected and unintelligible. We are all of us reluctant to unlearn our ways of making sense of the world, but think of all the life that might reveal itself to us if we tried. How much more might we learn about ourselves and others?

NOTES

INTRODUCTION

A portion of the introduction appeared in "The Rough Trade of US Imperialism," *Journal of Homosexuality* 59:7 (2012): 1081–86. Reprinted by permission of Taylor & Francis.

1 Holland 3.
2 In a January 1, 2012, article for the *Chronicle of Higher Education* in which he contemplates "the end of queer theory," Michael Warner locates "trans studies, postcolonial queer studies, [and] queer race studies" as younger adaptations of a foundational queer theory. Although Warner argues that these developments situate queer theory in the past, he similarly, if more grandly, fixes queer theory of the early 1990s as an originary past, casting trans, postcolonial, and queer race critiques as rebellious, oedipal children. He distinguishes these movements as being tied to political constituencies, implicitly situating an originary queer theory of the 1990s as the pure subjectless critique. Queer of Color Critique, for instance, might challenge Warner's genealogy, tracing its origins to multiple sources, including women of color feminism, as elaborated in texts such as "The Combahee River Collective Statement" of 1977 and *This Bridge Called My Back: Writing by Radical Women of Color*, edited by Cherríe Moraga and Gloria Anzaldúa, originally published in 1981. The reissue by SUNY Press of a fourth edition of *Bridge* in 2015 complicates Warner's framing of the "end of queer theory," but only if we allow for multiple genealogies of how we understand "queer" (as well as "theory").
3 According to linguist Paul Baker, the term "trade" can be used broadly to mean simply "male sex." However, I am most interested here in its historical and continued usage to specify working-class and presumably straight men. Baker elaborates,

> Trade, which is broadly a euphemism for a casual sexual partner, dates back to the Molly words of the eighteenth century, and has taken on several shades of meaning. Earlier, in the seventeenth century, "the trade" was used as slang to refer to prostitution, whereas, by the twentieth century, "trade" was used by the Navy to refer to the submarine service. Common Polari usages implied a gay pickup, or a gay prostitute. It can also be used collectively to refer to male prostitutes or gay men as a group. . . . [R]ough trade . . . is a particular kind of homosexual—one who

perhaps becomes violent or demands money after sex. *Trade* can also refer to a heterosexual man who is available for casual sex, usually only allowing himself to be fellated, or taking the active role in anal intercourse. (*Polari*, 193)

4 Puar, *Terrorist Assemblages*, 77.

5 Eng, Halberstam, and Muñoz 1.

6 Sedgwick, *Epistemology of the Closet*, 49.

7 "As wage labor spread and production became socialized, then, it became possible to release sexuality from the "imperative" to procreate. Ideologically, heterosexual expression came to be a means of establishing intimacy, promoting happiness, and experiencing pleasure. In divesting the household of its economic independence and fostering the separation of sexuality from procreation, capitalism has created conditions that allow some men and women to organize a personal life around their erotic/emotional attraction to their own sex. It has made possible the formation of urban communities of lesbians and gay men and, more recently, of a politics based on sexual identity." (D'Emilio 470)

8 Baker, *Polari*, 104.

9 Baker, *Fantabulosa*, 58.

10 Casarino 61.

11 Boym 4.

12 For a discussion of gay cloning, see Richard Meyer's "Warhol's Clones."

13 Agathangelou, Bassichis, and Spira 139.

14 Sharon Holland's work on the "erotic life of racism" is useful here, as is the writing of Agathangelou, Bassichis, and Spira on affective economies: "By 'affective economies,' we refer to the circulation and mobilization of feelings of desire, pleasure, fear, and repulsion utilized to seduce all of us into the fold of the state—the various ways in which we become invested emotionally, libidinally, and erotically in global capitalism's mirages of safety and inclusion" (122).

15 We might think of Robert McRuer's caution against neoliberalism's predatory nature as a caution too about the legacies of global capitalism from which neoliberalism emerges. Building on work by Gérard Duménil and Dominique Lévy, McRuer writes, "it [neoliberalism] is predatory on the liberatory energies our movements have generated, the resistant identifications we shape, the resources we might access, and the radical openness to alternative futures that (appears to be a common desire) across progressive movements." See McRuer.

16 A term first coined by Lisa Duggan, "homonormativity" is defined by Puar as a formation that "ties the recognition of homosexual subjects, both legally and representationally, to the national and transnational political agendas of U.S. imperialism" (*Terrorist Assemblages*, 9).

17 Massad.

18 As Roderick Ferguson defines it, "Queer of color analysis . . . interrogates social formations as the intersections of race, gender, sexuality, and class with particular

interest in how those formations correspond with and diverge from nationalist ideals and practices" (149).

19 For discussion of "perpetrator perspective," see Freeman.

CHAPTER 1. THE QUEER AFTERLIFE OF *BILLY BUDD*

1 See Morrison.

2 When I presented an early version of this chapter at the American Studies Association (November 19, 2010), Andrea Smith, for instance, argued that my analysis should begin in 1492.

3 See Roth 108.

4 "The writing of a Proust or a James would be exemplary here: projects precisely of *nonce* taxonomy, of the making and unmaking and *re*making and redissolution of hundreds of odd and new categorical imaginings concerning all the kinds it may take to make up a world" (*Epistemology*, 23).

5 Greven.

6 For a discussion of the influence of phrenology on the writing of *Billy Budd* and relevant titles in Melville's library, see McGlamery.

7 Scorza 6.

8 Critics have characterized this dispute as one of "irony versus acceptance." David Greven summarizes these competing positions with the following questions: "Is *Billy Budd* a final acquiescence to the forces of legality, jurisprudence, social control, orderliness, rationalism—in other words, a conservative testament of acceptance and affirmation? Or is it a harrowing indictment of the dehumanization of man in a 'civilized' era, a work of the bitterest irony—in other words, a testament of resistance?" See Greven.

9 Tellingly, Melville uses the French word "*chevalier*" to specify the nature of Claggart's criminality, at once reinforcing the charge of his foreignness but also suggesting a particularly treacherous character considering that the story is set during the French Wars. As is typical of Melville, use of the term "*chevalier*" introduces several more contradictions. If the term designates the master-at-arms as a criminal, it also suggests, ironically, a chivalrous character, noble birth, and—perhaps most contradictory given Claggart's office and the way the narrative distinguishes him from both the sailors and other officers—one who welcomes the opportunity for military service.

10 The distinction between savages and barbarians, made by Thomas Arnold and others, may be relevant here. According to Arnold, "*savages* could never civilize themselves, but *barbarians* I think might" (Stanley 246).

CHAPTER 2. "GOING TO MEET THE MAN" IN ABU GHRAIB

1 There are even fewer attempts to read that collection of stories itself as a text. And I don't attempt to do that here, but I do think it's important work. For a rare instance of such an approach, see Matt Brim's essay, "Papa's Baby:

Impossible Paternity in *Going to Meet the Man*," in which the author analyzes three of the collection's stories as "recursive and interlocking texts . . . bound together . . . by their cumulative power to defamiliarize, to make strange, whiteness." Brim reads Baldwin's opus, rightly I think, as an expedition into the heart of whiteness.

2 Sante.

3 Puar, *Terrorist Assemblages*, 85–86.

4 Carby, "A Strange and Bitter Crop."

5 See Dayan.

6 For an excellent and more deeply psychoanalytic reading of the oedipal complex in the story, and one that draws conclusions different from mine, see Yukari Yanagino's dissertation. Yanagino also uses the story to challenge the resistance within psychoanalysis to theorizing race.

7 Baldwin 229.

8 Even before this scene, Jesse associates Otis with the mysteries of sex, investing his eight-year-old friend with an innate carnal knowledge: "He had grown accustomed, for the solution of such mysteries, to go to Otis. He felt that Otis knew everything" (243).

9 For Yanagino, the father's tongue functions in Jesse's imagination as a fantasmatic substitute for the penis: "Although he [Jesse] is unable to see his father's penis, when he sees his father's tongue, he sees it fantasmatically. In other words, he sees his father's tongue as penis" (195).

10 According to Yanagino, the father's refusal to punish Jesse's erection (with the threat of castration) constitutes "homosexual bonding." She argues that "the enigmatic effect of this moment in his psychic world instills the understanding in Jesse that even though he maintains his infantile erotic wishes towards his parents, his father will not punish him by castrating him" (226). For Yanagino, the secret that Jesse's father shares with his son is that white men will not be castrated; castration is reserved for the black male body. This secret "forms an empathetic, homoerotic bonding relationship with his father" (225).

11 For an account where this disowned desire and subsequent rape fantasy prove formative as well of white femininity, see Joan Riviere's "Womanliness as Masquerade." Interestingly, although this is a much celebrated text for its value to queer and feminist applications of performativity, readings of Riviere's essay habitually forgo analysis of the text's value to understanding racialization.

12 Carby, *Reconstructing Womanhood*, 39.

13 American Civil Liberties Union.

14 Tétreault 34.

15 Hersh.

CHAPTER 3. THE GLOBAL TASTE FOR QUEER

1 See Belnap and Fernández.

2 "Blond nation of the continent . . . bilious, dark-skinned men." Except for the instances where I disagree with her rendition of specific words or phrases, I will refer to Elinor Randall's translation of "Nuestra América." See José Martí, "Our America," trans. Elinor Randall, in Martí, *Our America*, 84–94.

3 Stratton.

4 Santi 413.

5 For example, he observes that "[n]o mention is made of AIDS in the film, despite its themes; the disease seems not to be an issue in Cuba." Stratton erroneously globalizes his association of HIV/AIDS with homosexuality, but, even more significantly if we wish to situate the film within its local particularities, it is set in 1979, two years *before* HIV/AIDS is identified by epidemiologists, and was produced in 1993, two years *after* Cuba's controversial implementation of an AIDS quarantine.

6 Robbins 5.

7 Ortiz, "Docile Bodies," 91.

8 Nero 48–49.

9 Hamilton 48.

10 "The film's enthusiastic reception by the Havana public . . . offers conclusive proof of the erosion of traditional homophobia within Cuban society but not necessarily within the state. For the Cuban Film Institute, ICAIC, was prepared to support the project of brilliant, apparently heterosexual directors Tomás Gutiérrez Alea and Juan Carlos Tabío, but it simultaneously blocked all attempts by its gay members, some of whom are almost as accomplished, to produce work with gay themes." (Lumsden 195)

11 Smith, *Vision Machines*, 77–78.

12 For discussion of the film's labor toward reconciliation, see Santi.

13 Rickey.

14 See Retamar.

15 Ortiz, "Revolution's Other Histories," 40.

16 Paz, *Strawberry and Chocolate*, 52.

17 Bejel xvii.

18 See Sommerville.

19 José Martí, "Nuestra América," in *Sus Mejores Paginas*, 92.

20 Quiroga 139.

21 "Echar, bullendo y rebotando, por las venas, la sangre natural del país! En pie, con los ojos alegres de los trabajadores, se saludan, de un pueblo a otro, los hombres nuevos americanos."

22 A'ness 88.

23 Smith, "The Language of Strawberry," 31.

24 John Hess likewise observes that "[s]ome, perhaps many, Cubans saw and appreciated the film as a wider critique of the Cuban government's narrow-minded, puritan control of cultural and personal life" (120).

25 Behar 401.

26 Balaisis 37.

27 Balaisis explains, "the cinematic text provides a crucial window and forum for public expression, however subtle it may be. For them [Stephanie and James Donald] publicness may be witnessed in the oblique visual and textual cues provided by the film itself, which they refer to as symbolic public space" (37).

28 "[W]hile *Strawberry and Chocolate* had received a wide audience and much acclaim outside Cuba and had been broadcast regularly on 'Cubavisión Internacional,' residents on the island had only had access to the film in cinemas. These accounts challenge the 'official version' of the history of *Strawberry and Chocolate*, replacing the widely accepted tale of rectification and progress with one of caution and censorship. In the spring of 2008, no doubt in reply to these public criticisms, the film was broadcast on domestic television for the first time." (Hamilton 135–36)

CHAPTER 4. YOU CAN HAVE MY BROWN BODY AND EAT IT, TOO!

An earlier version of chapter 4 appeared as "You Can Have My Brown Body and Eat It, Too," *Social Text* 23:3–4 (2005): 171–91. Reprinted by permission of Duke University Press.

1 For a cogent examination of how whiteness functions in the United States as property, see Cheryl I. Harris's essay, "Whiteness as Property."

2 I identify Montez as Puerto Rican and Davis as black to illustrate the conference's race politics. However, I do so with some hesitation, as each figure's race/ethnic identity needs further complicating in order to investigate the place of racialized desire in forming racial, ethnic, and sexual identities (and vice versa). Vaginal Creme Davis, for example, has produced work exploring her Chicana heritage. José Muñoz records Davis's history (or "legend"):

> According to Davis's own self-generated legend, her existence is the result of an illicit encounter between her then forty-five-year-old African American mother and her father, who was, at the time, a twenty-one-year-old Mexican American. Davis has often reported that her parents only met once, when she was conceived under a table during a Ray Charles concert at the Hollywood Palladium in the early 1960s. (Muñoz, *Disidentifications,* 95)

In the case of Montez, the category "Puerto Rican" can designate not only a national origin but also a racial identification; in either case, what "Puerto Rican" means is contingent also on historical context, place, and usage. I do not know for certain that Montez self-identified as "Puerto Rican," nor do I take for granted that the meaning of such an identification necessarily remains constant over one's lifetime.

3 Judith Butler and Biddy Martin, "Cross-Identifications," *Diacritics* 24 (1994): 3.

4 See Biddy Martin.

5 Butler and Martin 3.

6 Harris, "Whiteness as Property," 277.

7 Hereafter cited as "the USA PATRIOT Act," the bill—passed on October 24, 2001, by the 107th Congress—is officially titled the "Uniting and Strengthening America by Providing Appropriate Tools Required to Intercept and Obstruct Terrorism Act of 2001."

8 For a discussion of the U.S. military's "warrior caste," see Halbfinger and Holmes.

9 The treatment of Iraqi prisoners of war and the histories of sexual humiliation of racially oppressed people in the United States are profoundly linked. The Abu Ghraib photos, like so many from the culture of lynching, function as postcards from a racial front. U.S. race ideology persists onto a world stage. Official responses to Abu Ghraib protect the race secrets of U.S. dominant and military cultures, which dictate the specifically sexual nature of the torture—at once sadistically homophobic and homoerotic. I want to underscore here cosmopolitanism's need for military occupation as a means of colonizing spaces for its material and imagined travels.

10 I am paraphrasing Kendall Thomas's invaluable formulation: "Race is a verb."

11 All race categories are, of course, regardless of their juridico-medical fixity, constitutively ambiguous. That ambiguity is relentlessly recuperated or even revoked by dominant culture (i.e., the one-drop rule, border patrol, determinations of dangerousness), but this same ambiguity perhaps also presents us with fertile ruptures in U.S. histories of systemic race oppression.

12 John Ashcroft's policy requiring male immigrants originating from any of twenty selected countries to register and periodically "check in" demonstrates how forms of governmentality adapt to endlessly and opportunistically mine the racial ambiguity of "brown," all the while professing to demystify it.

13 Hughes 6.

14 Quoted in Puar, "Circuits of Queer Mobility," 102.

15 Ibid., 104.

16 This chapter focuses on a troublesome gay cosmopolitanism that I argue characterizes establishmentarian queer theorizing. The 2003 Gay Shame conference provides the primary text for this investigation; however, Gay Shame occasioned various ruptures among the community of theorists, artists, and activists present. For the purposes of this chapter, I am interested in how a queer community (despite numerous assertions about the fictitiousness of such community) was violently consolidated at Gay Shame, perhaps even by the very ruptures I mention. However, I do want to emphasize that Gay Shame witnessed not only predictable alignments of power but also numerous realignments, especially realigned masculinities. By focusing so exclusively on the construction of a gay male cosmopolitanism, this chapter risks participating in the routine

"subordination of alternative masculinities" that Judith Halberstam explores in her writing. What Halberstam describes as "lesbian counterproductions of female masculinity" needs to be appraised vis-à-vis Gay Shame, just as any potential complicity with dominant white masculinity requires appraisal. See Halberstam, *Female Masculinity*.

17 The reference (made at the conference by Ellis Hanson) is to Eve Sedgwick's distinction between paranoid and reparative criticism in her essay "Paranoid Reading and Reparative Reading; or, You're So Paranoid, You Probably Think This Essay Is about You." See Sedgwick, *Touching Feeling*. I worry that Sedgwick's essay endorses the kind of unimaginative listening that protects a closed core of queer theory from unwelcome troubling. More significant, Sedgwick adopts the category "paranoid" without a consideration of the gendered and raced history of such pathologizing categories as they have been variously enlisted within the humanities and social sciences and within the everyday life of the academy in ways contingent on—yet exceeding—their clinical etiologies. If I may risk a generalization, an "essentialism" even: All colored academics know that expression of sincere yet dubious concern, that unmistakable "are you sure you're not just being too sensitive?" look on the faces of their trusted, good white liberal friends. Even when the question is articulated in that familiar, practiced tone of aggressive apprehension, it is never really a question at all, but rather an impervious accusation of paranoia. My other concern with Sedgwick's recycling of paranoia is its presumption that any criticism deemed "paranoid" was necessarily and naively directed at author intention, that is, Sedgwick means me, or my kind, harm. This ultimately provides a way to deflect criticism that confronts how words and images actually do injure people. It also minimizes the author's accountability with respect to the effects of her words. Witnessing too often the devastation exacted by the Left's "good intentions," I do not care much about the question of good or bad intentions. As a critic, I am concerned with the effects of words and images on lives. I do, however, also direct my analysis to motivation, which I understand as a very different problem from intention. Motivation introduces different questions from the more atomistic problem of intention. Rather than positing individual consciousness as its end, the question of motivation looks to the dynamics of group identity formation and the fantasies and desires they generate.

18 Crimp 57.

19 Hanson contested this point. However, he conceded that he might have been too ironic (hence, my misunderstanding).

20 Hanson disagreed, characterizing the "move" to trauma as "easy."

21 Erikson 184. For a discussion of race shame and the value of trauma theory to theorizing black identity, see Bouson.

22 I reiterate that the conference also suggested numerous alternative identity alignments. I also want to emphasize that my thinking on gay shame, race, and

institutional queer theory benefited immeasurably from the papers, performances, and interventions by conference speakers and audience members,
including George Chauncey, Deborah Gould, Judith Halberstam, Lisa Henderson,
Holly Hughes, Liza Johnson, Joan Lipkin, Esther Newton, Nolan O'Dell, Elaine
Roth, Bill St. Amant, Sarita See, Carroll Smith-Rosenberg, and many others.
23 Mercer 189.
24 Muñoz 110.
25 Halperin and Traub 30.
26 Halberstam, "Shame and White Gay Masculinity," 231.

CHAPTER 5. GAY COWBOYS CLOSE TO HOME
An earlier version of chapter 5 appeared in *Reading Brokeback Mountain: Essays on the Story and the Film*, ed. Jim Stacy (Jefferson, NC: McFarland, 2007). Reprinted by permission of McFarland & Company.
1 Proulx 262.
2 Ryan James Kim, "Not a Gay Movie," *Advocate.com,* December 9, 2005. Available at http://www.advocate.com/exclusive_detail_ektid23265.asp
3 See for example, Manohla Dargis, "Masculinity and Its Discontents in Marlboro Country," *New York Times*, December 18, 2005, 13; Neva Chonin, "Midnight Cowboys," *San Francisco Chronicle*, December 18, 2005, 14; Meghan Daum, "A Breakthrough Called *Brokeback*," *Los Angeles Times*, January 7, 2006, B17; Paul Gessel, "*Brokeback Mountain* Is 'Just Another Chick Flick,'" *Ottawa Citizen*, December 19, 2005, D3; Caryn James, "The Winner Is Only Acting Gay," *New York Times*, November 20, 2005, sec. 2:1; David Leavitt, "Men in Love: Is *Brokeback Mountain* a Gay Film?" *Slate,* December 8, 2005, http://www.slate.com/id/2131865; Adam Mars-Jones, "Out Takes," *Observer*, December 18, 2005, 1; Joanna Weiss, "Considering the Source: *Brokeback Mountain* Turns a Short Story into a Hollywood First," *Boston Globe*, December 11, 2005, N13; John Wirt, "*Brokeback Mountain* Tells an Unconventional Love Story," *Advocate*, January 13, 2006, 17.
4 Quoted in Dargis, supra note 3.
5 Halberstam, *In a Queer Time and Place*, 1.
6 Quoted in Dargis, supra note 3.
7 Leavitt, supra note 3.
8 Mars-Jones, supra note 3.
9 Trebay sec. 9:1.
10 Ryan James Kim (supra note 2), for example, pronounces Ennis's cowardice: "By the end of the film it's the expressive Jack we consider brave and the silent Ennis we find cowardly." Such criticism ignores more complicated queer identifications with Ennis, including class-based identifications.
11 According to Foucault, "the notion of 'sex' made it possible to group together, in an artificial unity, anatomical elements, biological functions, conducts, sensations,

and pleasures, and it enabled one to make use of this fictitious unity as a causal
principle, an omnipresent meaning" (154).

12 Trebay sec 9:1.

13 Ibid.

14 Halberstam, *In a Queer Time and Place*, 35.

15 Ibid. 25–26.

16 Wirt, supra note 3.

17 Quoted in Dargis, supra note 3.

18 Halberstam, *In a Queer Time and Place*, 10.

19 Slatta 6.

20 In English, "cowman" is in fact reserved for the landowning rancher, in contrast
    to the unpropertied "cowboy." See Wagner.

21 Packard 3.

22 Manohla Dargis, supra note 3, comments on the controversy over the film's
    authenticity: "A lightning rod for attention even before it opened, the film has
    earned plaudits from critics' groups along with predictable sneers, and provoked
    argument over its gay bona fides."

23 Steinberg 58.

24 Halberstam, *In a Queer Time and Place*, 27.

25 Leavitt.

26 Packard 13.

27 Wagner 21–22.

28 Wagner 95.

29 As Wagner notes,

    "Cowboy" was, for a number of years, a pejorative word that did not
    make its way into polite vocabulary. . . . [T]he earliest dictionaries that
    were available in which the word cowboy is defined as someone who
    tends cattle are in the 1888 edition of *A New English Dictionary on
    Historical Principles* and the 1901 edition of *The American Dictionary of
    English*. (95)

30 Bersani 31.

31 Johnson 15–16.

BIBLIOGRAPHY

Agathangelou, Anna M., M. Daniel Bassichis, and Tamara L. Spira. "Intimate Investments: Homonormativity, Global Lockdown, and the Seductions of Empire." *Radical History Review* 100 (2008): 120–43.

Alexander, M. Jacqui. "Erotic Autonomy as a Politics of Decolonization: An Anatomy
of Feminist and State Practice." In *Feminist Genealogies, Colonial Legacies, Democratic Futures*, ed. M. Jacqui Alexander and Chandra Talpade Mohanty, 63–100.
New York: Routledge, 1997.

———. *Pedagogies of Crossing: Meditations on Feminism, Sexual Politics, Memory, and
the Sacred*. Durham, NC: Duke University Press, 2006.

American Civil Liberties Union. "Appeals Court Orders Defense Department to
Release Detainee Abuse Photos in ACLU Lawsuit." *American Civil Liberties Union*,
September 22, 2008, Web. Available at https://www.aclu.org/national-security/
appeals-court-orders-defense-department-release-detainee-abuse-photos-aclu-
lawsuit

A'ness, Francine. "A Lesson in Synthesis: Nation Building and Images of a 'New Cuba'
in *Fresa y chocolate*." *Lucero: A Journal of Iberian & Latin American Studies* 7
(Spring 1996): 86–98.

Anzaldúa, Gloria. *Borderlands/La Frontera: The New Mestiza*. San Francisco: Aunt Lute
Books, 2012.

Axel, Brian Keith. "The Diasporic Imaginary." *Public Culture* 14:2 (Spring 2002):
411–28.

Baker, Paul. *Fantabulosa: A Dictionary of Polari and Gay Slang*. London: Continuum,
2002.

———. *Polari: The Lost Language of Gay Men*. London: Routledge, 2002.

Balaisis, Nicholas. "Cuba, Cinema, and the Post-Revolutionary Public Sphere." *Cana-
dian Journal of Film Studies/Revue Canadienne d'Etudes Cinématographiques* 19:2
(Fall 2010): 26–42.

Baldwin, James. *Going to Meet the Man*. New York: Vintage International, 1995.

Behar, Ruth. "Queer Times in Cuba." In *Bridges to Cuba/Puentes a Cuba*, ed. Ruth
Behar, 394–415. Ann Arbor: University of Michigan Press, 1995.

Bejel, Emilio. *Gay Cuban Nation*. Chicago: University of Chicago Press, 2001.

Belnap, Jeffrey, and Raúl Fernández. *José Martí's "Our America": From National to
Hemispheric Cultural Studies*. Durham, NC: Duke University Press, 1998.

Bersani, Leo. "Sexuality and Aesthetics." *October* 28 (1984): 27–42.

Bouson, J. Brooks. *Quiet As It's Kept: Shame, Trauma, and Race in the Novels of Toni Morrison*. Albany: State University of New York Press, 2000.

Boym, Svetlana. *The Future of Nostalgia*. New York: Basic Books, 2002.

Brecht, Stefan. *Queer Theatre*. New York: Methuen, 1985.

Brim, Matt. "Papa's Baby: Impossible Paternity in *Going to Meet the Man*." *Journal of Modern Literature* 30:1 (Fall 2006): 173–98.

Bronski, Michael, Terri Ginsberg, Roy Grundmann, Kara Keeling, Liora Moriel, Yasmin Nair, and Kirsten Moana Thompson, "Queer Film and Media Pedagogy." *GLQ: A Journal of Lesbian and Gay Studies* 12:1 (2006): 117–34.

Butler, Judith, and Biddy Martin. "Cross-Identifications." *Diacritics* 24 (1994): 3.

Carby, Hazel. *Reconstructing Womanhood: The Emergence of the Afro-American Woman Novelist*. New York: Oxford University Press, 1987.

———. "A Strange and Bitter Crop: The Spectacle of Torture." *Open Democracy*, October 10, 2004. Available at https://www.opendemocracy.net/media-abu_ghraib/article_2149.jsp

Casarino, Cesar. *Modernity at Sea: Melville, Marx, Conrad in Crisis*. Minneapolis: University of Minnesota Press, 2002.

Crimp, Douglas. "Mario Montez, For Shame." In *Regarding Sedgwick: Essays on Queer Culture and Critical Theory*, ed. Stephen M. Barber and David L. Clark, 57–70. New York: Routledge, 2002.

Dayan, Colin. *The Story of Cruel and Unusual*. Cambridge: MIT Press, 2007.

D'Emilio, John. "Capitalism and Gay Identity." In *The Lesbian and Gay Studies Reader*, ed. Henry Abelove, Michèlle Aina Barale, and David M. Halperin, 467–76. New York: Routledge, 1993.

Donald, James, and Stephanie Hemelryk Donald. "The Publicness of Cinema." In *Reinventing Film Studies*, ed. Christine Gledhill and Linda Williams, 114–29. London: Arnold Publishers, 2000.

Duggan, Lisa. *The Twilight of Equality? Neoliberalism, Cultural Politics, and the Attack on Democracy*. Boston: Beacon, 2003.

Eng, David L., Judith Halberstam, and José Esteban Muñoz. Introduction, "What's Queer about Queer Studies Now." *Social Text* 23 (2005): 1–17.

Erikson, Kai. "Notes on Trauma and Community." In *Trauma: Explorations in Memory*, ed. Cathy Caruth, 183–99. Baltimore, MD: Johns Hopkins University Press, 1995.

Ferguson, Roderick. *Aberrations in Black: Toward a Queer of Color Critique*. Minneapolis: University of Minnesota Press, 2003.

Foucault, Michel. *The History of Sexuality*. Volume 1, *An Introduction*. New York: Vintage, 1990.

Freeman, Alan. "Legitimizing Racial Discrimination through Antidiscrimination Law: A Critical Review of Supreme Court Doctrine." *Minnesota Law Review* 62 (1977–78): 1049.

Gabilondo, Joseba. "Like Blood for Chocolate, Like Queers for Vampires: Border and Global Consumption in Rodríguez, Tarantino, Arau, Esquivel, and Troyano (Notes on Baroque, Camp, Kitsch, and Hybridization)." In *Queer Globalizations: Citizenship and the Afterlife of Colonialism*, ed. Arnaldo Cruz-Malavé and Martin Manalansan, 236–64. New York: New York University Press, 2002.

Gardiner, James. *Who's a Pretty Boy, Then? One Hundred and Fifty Years of Gay Life in Pictures*. London: Serpent's Tail, 1997.

Goldberg, Jonathan. *Sodometries: Renaissance Texts, Modern Sexualities*. Stanford, CA: Stanford University Press, 1992.

———. "Sodomy in the New World: Anthropologies Old and New." *Social Text* 29 (1991): 46–56.

Greven, David. "Flesh in the Word: *Billy Budd, Sailor*, Compulsory Homosociality, and the Uses of Queer Desire." *Genders* 37 (2003). Available at http://www.genders.org/g37/g37_greven.html

Halberstam, Judith. *Female Masculinity*. Durham, NC: Duke University Press, 1998.

———. *In a Queer Time and Place: Transgender Bodies, Subcultural Lives*. New York: New York University Press, 2005.

———. "Shame and White Gay Masculinity." *Social Text* 23:3–4 (1984–1985): 219–33.

Halbfinger, David M., and Steven A. Holmes. "A Nation at War: The Troops; Military Mirrors a Working-Class America." *New York Times*, March 30, 2003.

Halperin, David M., and Valerie Traub. "Beyond Gay Pride." In *Gay Shame*, ed. David M. Halperin and Valerie Traub, 3–40. Chicago: University of Chicago Press, 2010.

Hamilton, Carrie. *Sexual Revolutions in Cuba: Passion, Politics, and Memory*. Chapel Hill: University of North Carolina Press, 2012.

Hanson, Ellis. "The Future's Eve: Reparative Reading after Sedgwick." *South Atlantic Quarterly* 110:1 (Winter 2011): 101–19.

———. "Teaching Shame." In *Gay Shame*, ed. David M. Halperin and Valerie Traub, 132–64. Chicago: University of Chicago Press, 2010.

Harris, Cheryl I. "Whiteness as Property." In *Critical Race Theory: The Key Writings That Formed the Movement*, ed. Kimberlé Crenshaw, Neil Gotanda, Gary Peller, and Kendall Thomas, 276–91. New York: New Press, 1995.

Hersh, Seymour M. "Chain of Command: How the Department of Defense Mishandled the Disaster at Abu Ghraib." *New Yorker*, May 17, 2004. Available at http://www.newyorker.com/magazine/2004/05/17/chain-of-command-2

Hess, John. "*Strawberry and Chocolate*: Melodrama, Sex, and the Cuban Revolution." In *Jump Cut: A Review of Contemporary Media* 41 (May 1997): 119–25.

Hoad, Neville. "Arrested Development or the Queerness of Savages: Resisting Evolutionary Narratives of Difference." *Postcolonial Studies* 3:2 (2000): 133–58.

Holland, Sharon Patricia. *The Erotic Life of Racism*. Durham, NC: Duke University Press, 2012.

Hughes, Howard. "Holidays and Homosexual Identity." *Tourism Management* 18 (1997): 3–7.

Johnson, Barbara. *A World of Difference*. Baltimore, MD: Johns Hopkins University Press, 1988.

Leavitt, David. "Men in Love: Is *Brokeback Mountain* a Gay Film?" *Slate*, December 8, 2005. Available at http://www.slate.com/id/2131865

Lorde, Audre. "The Uses of the Erotic: The Erotic as Power." In *Sister Outsider: Essays and Speeches*, Audre Lorde, 53–59. New York: Crossing Press, 2007.

Lumsden, Ian. *Machos, Maricones, and Gays: Cuba and Homosexuality*. Philadelphia: Temple University Press, 1996.

Martí, José. "Our America." In *Our America: Writings on Latin America and the Struggle for Cuban Independence*, ed. Philip S. Foner, 84–94. New York: Monthly Review Press, 1977.

———. "Nuestra América." In *Sus Mejores Paginas*, ed. Raimundo Lazo, 87–93. México: Editorial Porrua, 1992.

Martin, Biddy. "Sexualities without Genders and Other Queer Utopias." *Diacritics* 24 (1994): 104–21.

Massad, Joseph. *Desiring Arabs*. Chicago: University of Chicago Press, 2007.

McGlamery, Tom. *Protest and the Body in Melville, Dos Passos, and Hurston*. New York: Routledge, 2004.

McRuer, Robert. "Cripping Queer Politics; or, The Dangers of Neoliberalism." *Scholar and Feminist Online* 10:1–10:2 (Fall 2011–Spring 2012).

Melville, Herman. *Billy Budd, Sailor*. Chicago: University of Chicago, 1962.

Mercer, Kobena. *Welcome to the Jungle: New Positions in Black Cultural Studies*. New York: Routledge, 1994.

Meyer, Richard. "Warhol's Clones." In *Negotiating Lesbian and Gay Subjects*, ed. Monica Doreknkapm and Richard Henke, 93–122. New York: Routledge, 1995.

Michaelsen, Scott. "Between Japanese American Internment and the USA PATRIOT Act: The Borderlands and the Permanent State of Racial Exception." *Aztlán: A Journal of Chicano Studies* 30:2 (Fall 2005): 87–111.

Moore, Patrick. "Gay Sexuality Shouldn't Become a Torture Device." *Newsday*, May 7, 2004, A51.

Moraga, Cherríe, and Gloria Anzaldúa, ed. *This Bridge Called My Back: Writings by Radical Women of Color*. Albany: State University of New York Press, 2015.

Morrison, Toni. *Playing in the Dark: Whiteness and the Literary Imagination*. New York: Vintage, 1993.

Muñoz, José Esteban. *Disidentifications: Queers of Color and the Performance of Politics*. Minneapolis: University of Minnesota Press, 1999.

———. "Race, Sex, and the Incommensurate: Gary Fisher with Eve Kosofsky Sedgwick." In *Queer Futures: Reconsidering Ethics, Activism, and the Political*, ed. Elahe Haschemi Yekani, Eveline Kilian, Beatrice Michaelis, 103–15. Burlington, VT: Ashgate, 2013.

Nero, Charles. "Diva Traffic and Male Bonding in Film: Teaching Opera, Learning Gender, Race, and Nation." *Camera Obscura* 19:2 (2004): 46–73.

Ortiz, Ricardo. "Docile Bodies, Volatile Texts: The Political Erotics of Cuban-Exile Prison Writing." *Annals of Scholarship* 12 (Fall 1998): 91–112.

———. "Revolution's Other Histories: The Sexual, Cultural, and Critical Legacies of Roberto Fernández Retamar's 'Caliban.'" *Social Text* no. 58 (Spring 1999): 33–58.

Packard, Chris. *Queer Cowboys: And Other Erotic Male Friendships in Nineteenth-Century American Literature.* New York: Palgrave/Macmillan, 2005.

Paz, Senel. *El lobo, el bosque, y el hombre nuevo.* Mexico: Ediciones Era, 2005.

———. *Strawberry and Chocolate.* Trans. Peter Bush. London: Bloomsbury, 1995.

Proulx, Annie. *Close Range: Wyoming Stories.* New York: Scribners, 1999.

Puar, Jasbir. "Circuits of Queer Mobility: Tourism, Travel, and Globalization." *GLQ* 8 (2002): 101–37.

———. *Terrorist Assemblages: Homonationalism in Queer Times.* Durham, NC: Duke University Press, 2007.

———. "A Transnational Feminist Critique of Queer Tourism." *Antipode* 34:5 (November 2002): 935–46.

Quiroga, José A. *Tropics of Desire: Interventions from Queer Latino America.* New York: New York University Press, 2000.

Retamar, Roberto Fernández. *Caliban and Other Essays.* Trans. Edward Baker. Minneapolis: University of Minnesota Press, 1989.

Rickey, Carrie. "Cuban Palette of Love and Politics." In *Philadelphia Inquirer*, February 10, 1995. Available at http://articles.philly.com/1995-02-10/entertainment/25704941_1_jorge-perugorria-strawberry-and-chocolate-vladimir-cruz Accessed July 10, 2013.

Riviere, Joan. "Womanliness as a Masquerade." In *Formations of Fantasy*, ed. Victor Burgin, James Donald, and Cora Kaplan, 35–44. New York: Methuen, 1986.

Robbins, Bruce. "Introduction Part I: Actually Existing Cosmopolitanism." In *Cosmopolitics: Thinking and Feeling beyond the Nation*, ed. Pheng Cheah and Bruce Robbins, 1–19. Minneapolis: University of Minnesota Press, 1998.

Roth, Marty. "The Disruption of Forms in *Billy Budd.*" *Boundary 2: An International Journal of Literature and Culture* 15:1–2 (Fall 1986): 107–22.

Sante, Luc. "Tourists and Torturers." *New York Times*, May 11, 2004. Available at http://www.nytimes.com/2004/05/11/opinion/tourists-and-torturers.html

Santi, Enrico Mario. "*Fresa y chocolate*: The Rhetoric of Cuban Reconciliation." *MLN* 113:2 (March 1998): 407–25.

Scorza, Thomas J. *In the Time before Steamships: Billy Budd, the Limits of Politics, and Modernity.* DeKalb: Northern Illinois University Press, 1979.

Sedgwick, Eve Kosofsky. *Epistemology of the Closet.* Berkeley: University of California Press, 1990.

———. *Touching Feeling: Affect, Pedagogy, Performativity.* Durham, NC: Duke University Press, 2003.

Slatta, Richard W. *Cowboys of the Americas.* New Haven, CT: Yale University Press, 1990.

Smith, Paul Julian. "The Language of Strawberry." *Sight and Sound*, December 1, 1994, 30–34.

———. *Vision Machines: Cinema, Literature, and Sexuality in Spain and Cuba, 1983–1998*. London: Verso, 1996.

Somerville, Siobhan. *Queering the Color Line: Race and the Invention of Homosexuality in American Culture*. Durham, NC: Duke University Press, 2000.

Stanley, Arthur Penrhyn. *The Life and Correspondence of Thomas Arnold, D.D., Late Headmaster of Rugby School, and Regius Professor of Modern History in the University of Oxford*. New York: Appleton, 1846.

Steinberg, Sybil. "E. Annie Proulx: An American Odyssey." *Publishers Weekly*, June 1996, 57–58.

Stout, David. "Bush Expresses 'Deep Disgust' over Abuse of Iraqi Prisoners." *New York Times*, April 30, 2004. Available at http://www.nytimes.com/2004/04/30/politics/30CND-BUSH.html

Stratton, David. "Review: *Fresa y Chocolate*." *Variety*, February 20, 1994. Available at http://variety.com/1994/film/reviews/fresa-y-chocolate-1200435771 Accessed July 11, 2013.

Tétreault, Mary Ann. "The Sexual Politics of Abu Ghraib: Hegemony, Spectacle, and the Global War on Terror." *NWSA Journal* 18:3 (Fall 2006): 33–50.

Thomas, Kendall. "The Eclipse of Reason: A Rhetorical Reading of Bowers v. Hardwick." *Virginia Law Review* 79:7 (October 1993): 1805–32.

Trebay, Guy. "Cowboys, Just Like in the Movies." *New York Times* (sec. 9:1), December 18, 2005.

Wagner, James. "Cowboy: Origin and Early Use of the Term." *West Texas Historical Association Yearbook* 63 (1987): 91–100.

Warner, Michael. "Queer and Then?" *Chronicle of Higher Education*, January 1, 2012. Available at http://chronicle.com/article/QueerThen-/130161 Accessed November 11, 2012.

Yanagino, Yukari. *Psychoanalysis and Literature: Perversion, Racism, and Language of Difference*. Dissertation, Rutgers University: 2008. Available at https://rucore.libraries.rutgers.edu/rutgers-lib/24076/pdf/1

INDEX

Abu Ghraib, 18–19; rape at, 52, 72, 74; scandal of, 66–67

Abu Ghraib photos: homophobia and homoeroticism in, 51, 68–75; lynching and, 49–50, 75; as pornography, 69–70; release of, 67

Acceptance, 155n8

Affective economies, 9–10, 154n14

Africanism, 25, 32

"African sailor," 17, 25, 29–33, 35–37, 43–44, 48

"Against Proper Objects" (Butler), 100

"Aguirre, Joe," 125, 137, 146–47, 149

AIDS, 121, 157n5

Alexander, M. Jacqui, 13–16

Allegory, 90–91

American Civil Liberties Union, 67

Analogy, 50–53, 70

Ancient Rome, 44–45

Antihomophobia, 34, 37, 72

Anti-identitarian model, 99

Anti-identity, 16, 104, 109, 118

Antipornography rhetoric, 69–70

Antiracist work, 1, 17

Anzaldúa, Gloria, 8, 153n2

"Ariel," 78, 83–85, 89–91

Art photography, 121

Assimilationists gay politics, 12, 16, 22, 120, 128, 145–47

Authenticity: in Billy Budd, Sailor, 29, 43; in Brokeback Mountain, 128, 136, 142–43, 162n22; of Montez, 111

Autochthonic mestizo (mestizo autóctono), 89

Axel, Brian, 73–74

Baker, Paul, 6, 153n3

Balaisis, Nicholas, 92–93, 158n27

Balboa, 13

Baldwin, James, 18, 49–50, 52–55, 57–60, 64–66

Barbarian, 31, 39, 44–47, 155n10

Beauty, 25, 29–32, 39, 44–45

Behar, Ruth, 92

Bejel, Emilio, 85–86, 89, 91

Bersani, Leo, 150

"Big Jim C.," 55–56

Billy Budd, Sailor: An Inside Narrative (Melville), 6–7, 17–18, 25–26, 41–44; Africanism of, 32; authenticity in, 29, 43; brown bodies in, 37–38; as historical novel, 42; irony in, 41–42, 155n8; modern gay male identity in, 30, 33; narrator of, 29, 40–43; whiteness and brownness in, 15

"Billy Budd," 15, 17; as barbarian, 45–47; eroticization of, 30–31; innocence of, 17, 31, 37–39, 44; stutter of, 15, 29–30, 47

Black bodies, 18, 51–55, 60–66, 103, 115–17, 156n10

Black Book (Mapplethorpe), 121, 123

Blackface, 32

Black men: desire for, 17–18, 30, 36, 53–54, 58–66, 115–17; torture of, 51, 56–57, 64

Blackness, 17, 31, 33, 64, 82, 115

Black penis, 63–64, 114–17

Black sexuality, 18, 64, 115, 117

Black women, 52–54, 57–58, 66, 151

ABOUT THE AUTHOR

Hiram Pérez is Assistant Professor of English at Vassar College.

CPSIA information can be obtained at www.ICGtesting.com
Printed in the USA
LVOW11s1024180816

500916LV00003B/117/P